EARLY DAYS
ON THE ROAD

LORD MONTAGU OF BEAULIEU AND G. N. GEORGANO

EARLY DAYS ON THE ROAD

An Illustrated History
1819–1941

UNIVERSE BOOKS
NEW YORK

Published in the United States of America in 1976
by Universe Books
381 Park Avenue South, New York, N.Y. 10016

Library of Congress Catalog Card Number: 76-8808
ISBN 0-87663-243-6

This book was designed and produced by
Rainbird Reference Books Limited
36 Park Street, London WIY 4DE
House Editor: Raymond Kaye
Designer: Trevor Vincent

The book was printed photolitho by
Ebenezer Baylis & Son Ltd, The Trinity Press,
Worcester, and London
The book was bound by Dorstel Press Ltd
Harlow

Printed in England

CONTENTS

FOREWORD

Most motoring and transport history books concentrate on a limited subject, but in *Early Days on the Road* we have set out to reflect the diversity of mechanically driven vehicles, including man-powered machines, that have been seen on the roads of the world over the past 150 years. History, of course, extends up to the present day, but we have chosen the not altogether arbitrary cut-off date of 1941 to close the book. This was the year that the United States of America entered World War II, when the development of passenger cars and other civilian vehicles ceased for several years, and pleasure motoring all but came to an end in European countries.

In the compilation of this book, the constant problem has been not what to include, but what had to be omitted if the book was to be kept to a reasonable size. Although many interesting photographs originally considered had to be rejected, the final selection does, we hope, give a representative picture of road transport in all its variety, from the tricycle to the 100-ton articulated lorry. In practically every case the photographs show the vehicles in their contemporary settings, with the exception of a few long-lived commercial vehicles that were still at work twenty or thirty years after they were made. Thus the book provides an incidental commentary on changing fashions in clothing and architecture, and on the state of the roads during the period.

The majority of photographs have been drawn from the archives of the National Motor Museum at Beaulieu, but we would like to acknowledge the help that certain specialist collectors have given, in particular Prince Marshall of *Old Motor Magazine*; Arthur Ingram and John Montville (British and American goods vehicles and fire engines); Albert E. Meier of the Motor Bus Society (American buses); and A. B. Demaus (bicycles). The following have also given valuable help in providing information: David Mondey, Albert E. Meier, Michael Sedgwick, Michael Worthington-Williams, and Stan Yost.

MONTAGU OF BEAULIEU
G. N. GEORGANO
October 1974

A typical tricycle of about 1880 with single front wheel and small stabilizing rear wheel. Steering was effected by the lever in the rider's right hand.

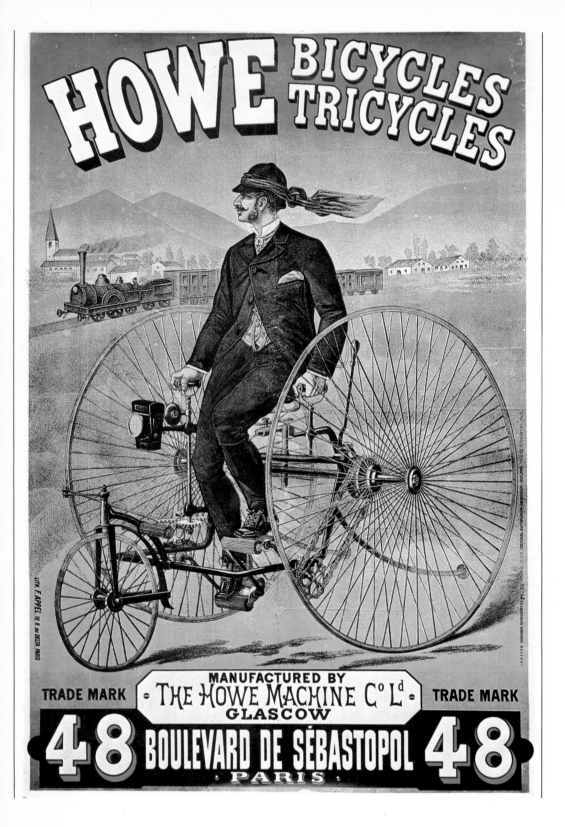

A late example (opposite) of the Ordinary bicycle with a front wheel considerably smaller than was common on these machines. The pneumatic tyres indicate a date after 1890, by which time the Ordinary had been almost entirely superseded by the Safety bicycle.

Imprimerie. PAUL DUPONT, 4, R. du Bouloi, Paris

One could hardly find a more blatant example of the advertising theme, 'Buy our product and succeed with the girls' than this poster for the Whitworth Safety bicycle, c. 1892.

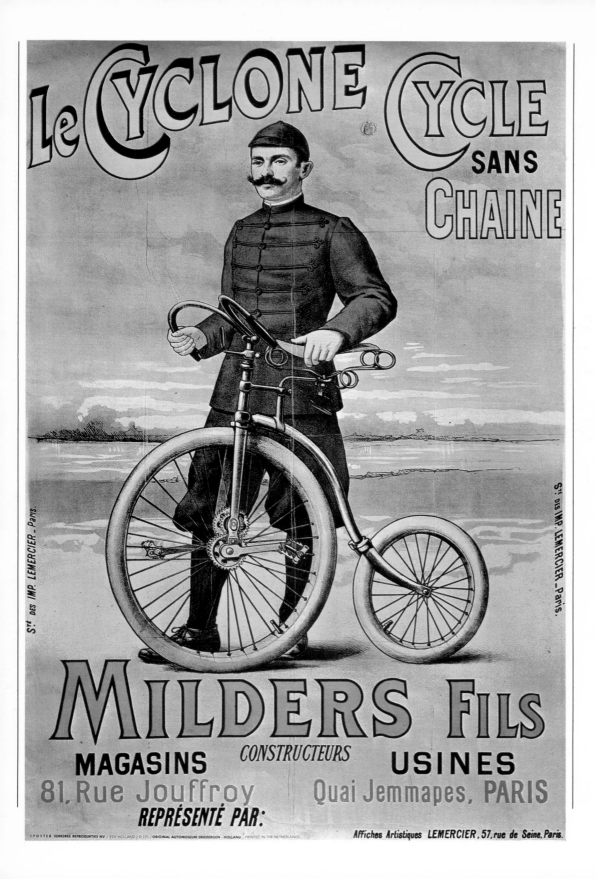

The caption to this French advertisement for Humber bicycles, c. 1895, 'See, my dear, when you ride a Humber you always have to wait for the others', foreshadows certain car advertising of the 1970s.

Early cars were sometimes displayed at bicycle shows, as indicated by this advertisement (below) for Audibert-Lavirotte cars, from 1896. The Lyon-built Audibert-Lavirotte was one of the earliest production cars in France but the company stayed in business only from 1894 to 1901, during which time it made about fifty cars.

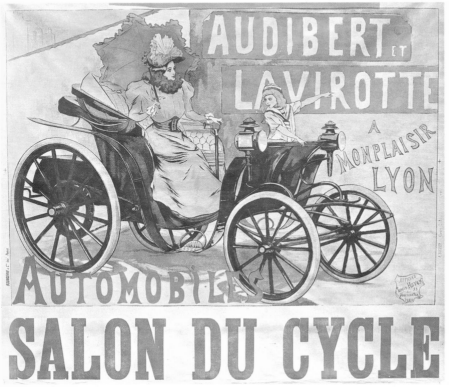

A typical early motorcycle was the single-cylinder belt-driven Rochet of about 1902

Motocyclette
Rochet
74. Rue de la FOLIE-REGNAULT
PARIS
P. CHAPELLIER
AFF. ARTISTIQUE P. CHAPELLIER. 12. Bd Magenta. PARIS

A Decauville four-seater tonneau.
This was a popular French make in its
earliest days, 1899–1900, when the
company produced a light car known by
the attractive term 'voiturelle'. By 1903,
the date of this advertisement, the products
were less distinctive, and it was
Henry Royce's dissatisfaction with his
Decauville that led him to make a car of
his own.

DECAUVILLE

Typical of French advertising at the turn of the century is this poster for Georges Richard cars and bicycles. Cars were made under the Georges Richard name from 1897 to 1903, when Henri Brasier joined the firm and the cars were sold as Richard-Brasiers.

Lanchesters were among the most individual car designs, their appearance characterized by very short bonnets as the rear part of the engine projected between driver and passenger. Other features were optional tiller steering (until 1911) and epicyclic gearboxes (until 1929). This print shows a 38hp six-cylinder tourer of 1913.

Leyland Heavy Pattern Steam Wagon and Trailer.

Two sides of Leyland's business as
publicized in 1914, a 6-ton steam wagon
with four-wheel trailer (inset), and a
petrol-engined 4-ton municipal tip wagon

Berliet advertising featured some beautifully evocative drawings by René Vincent of the company's vehicles in various major cities of the world.
The poster above shows a forward-control lorry in London; below is a limousine in Chicago. Both date from 1906.

The largest-engined and one of the most expensive cars ever made was the Fageol (opposite), built in Oakland, Cal., by a company later much better known for buses. Powered by a six-cylinder Hall-Scott engine of 13½ litres' capacity, the Fageol was offered in at least five different body styles, from 1916 to 1917 only. Prices were as high as $17,000.

CHICAGO

An unusual advertisement for the FIAT 501, best-selling product of the famous Italian company during the early 1920s. This dates from 1923.

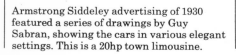

Armstrong Siddeley advertising of 1930 featured a series of drawings by Guy Sabran, showing the cars in various elegant settings. This is a 20hp town limousine.

A 1930 Buick Standard Six with British-built fabric saloon body known as the 'Regent'. Aviation backgrounds were popular in 1930s advertising.

A 1930 Sentinel GD6 steam wagon on pneumatic tyres

Opposite: six cylinders were still sufficiently unusual in light commercial vehicles for Chevrolet to make a feature of the fact in its 1930 advertising. The company used the same six-cylinder engine in both 12cwt (1344lb) and 30cwt (3360lb) chassis, this unit also serving in Chevrolet passenger cars.

THE
MORRIS-COMMERCIAL
INTERNATIONAL
TAXI-CAB

GMC OMNIBUSSAR

G.M.C. trucks and buses were popular in many countries of the world. This view of a six-cylinder coach comes from a 1930 Swedish catalogue. G.M.C. buses used Chevrolet or Buick engines at this time.

Opposite: catalogue cover showing one of the crop of new London taxicabs that appeared in the years 1929–30: the Morris-Commercial International, the first venture by this company into the cab trade. Internationals were widely used in provincial cities as well as in London.

8 CYLINDER 3.300 LITRE TYPE 49 CHASSIS FITTED WITH "CLOSE-COUPLED" 4 SEATER "SPORTSMAN" COUPÉ.

Above: catalogue picture of a 1932 Bugatti Type 49 close-coupled four-seater Sportsman coupé. The 3·3-litre straight-eight Type 49 was the ancestor of the Type 57 which formed the bulk of Bugatti production in the 1930s.

In 1932 the Jowett company was using the same flat-twin engine for its cars and light vans that it had begun production with in 1913. They came in two wheelbase lengths, 7ft 0in and 8ft 6in; the Simba long four-seater is illustrated. Jowett advertising featured a variety of slogans, from the simple 'Never Wears Out' to the more colourful 'The Pull of an Elephant and the Appetite of a Canary', and, perhaps best of all, 'With Spurs, would climb Trees'.

JOWETT CARS LIMITED · IDLE · BRADFORD · YORKS·

xvii

Left: the first European model of Ford was the 8hp 933cc Y type, introduced in 1932 and made in Britain, France and Germany. This detail from a catalogue illustration shows the two-door saloon in a fashionable setting usually associated with more expensive cars.

The Norton company capitalized on TT successes in its 1935 advertising (opposite). In 1934 Nortons won the Senior and Junior TTs, and the Club Team Prize for the fourth successive year.

A 348cc overhead-camshaft Velocette KTS model of 1936 (below left). The catalogue cover stresses the healthy companionship of the Great Outdoors.

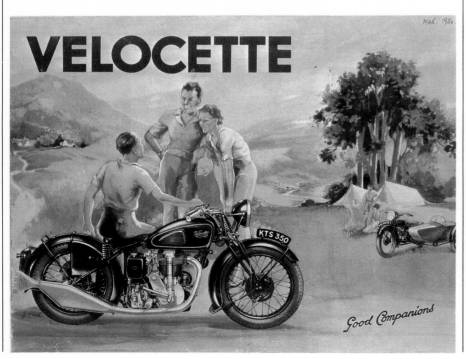

A 1934 B.S.A. 249cc single-cylinder motorcycle in the picturesque setting of Rye, Sussex

A 1937 Lincoln Zephyr V12 advertised in two-door sedan form. Other body styles of this period were a four-door sedan and a three-seater coupé.

Catalogue illustration of the 1938 Rolls-Royce Phantom III V12 with all-weather tourer coachwork. The Phantom III chassis cost £1900 and with this body the complete car was priced at £2820.

'He shall have chariots easier than air' was the slogan used by the makers of the Anglo-American Railton straight eight (right). Detail from the 1936 catalogue.

Catalogue illustration of the 1940 Indian
Sport Scout 45 with 45·44ci V-twin engine

SPRING FRAME
Indian Forty-Five
MODEL 641

Above: powered by the 'small' Ford V8 engine of 2·2 litres, the 25cwt Fordson in this catalogue illustration was a purely British product, not duplicated in the American or German Ford ranges, introduced for 1938 and made until the outbreak of World War II.

One of the most popular and successful FIAT models was the 1100, or 'Millecento'. The catalogue picture below shows the saloon and pick-up truck versions of 1939. The 1100 was also made as a six-light saloon, taxi and delivery van.

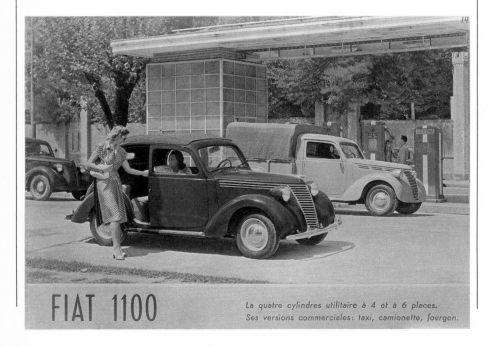

FIAT 1100

La quatre cylindres utilitaire à 4 et à 6 places. Ses versions commerciales: taxi, camionette, fourgon.

PASSENGER CARS

INTRODUCTION

The history of the passenger car dates back to the 1860s when a number of comparatively light steam carriages were made, in Britain and in the United States. Earlier road-going vehicles had been buses for up to twenty-two passengers, and their designers were apparently more interested in commercial operation than in private transportation, but the machines of such men as Thomas Rickett in England and Walter Dudgeon and Sylvester Roper in America were specifically planned as privately owned carriages seating not more than four or five passengers. Although Rickett succeeded in selling three of his carriages, and demonstrated one to Queen Victoria and Prince Albert, on the whole the early inventors had no commercial success, and hampered by restrictive legislation, most of them built no more than one car each. In the 1880s there was a resurgence of experiment, and this time it bore fruit in the form of cars actually made for sale. Credit for this is usually given to the internal-combustion engine as developed by Nikolaus August Otto and applied to vehicles by Karl Benz and Gottlieb Daimler, but the steam cars of de Dion-Bouton and Serpollet were much more refined and practical than their predecessors had been, and even if the petrol engine had never been invented, it is probable that a motor industry based on steam would have been well established by the mid-1890s. Indeed, in America steam cars did outsell internal-combustion ones from 1898 to 1902, thanks to their cheapness and freedom from the bugbear of gear changing.

The leading designs in Europe were the German Benz and French Panhard, and up to 1898 more Benzes were sold than any other make of car in the world. Most of these were the Velo model, a simple single-cylinder car with a top speed of about 18mph, which was as reliable as any car of that time. It had a rear-mounted horizontal engine and belt drive, features which Benz persisted with long after they had become outmoded. The car that made the Benz obsolete almost overnight was the front-engined Panhard of 1891. This has often been called the ancestor of the modern car, for it embodied several features that were to become standard practice in car design until comparatively recent years, when unorthodoxy has become more evident. The V-twin engine was mounted at the front of the chassis under a bonnet, and drove via a four-speed sliding pinion gear system and double chains to the rear wheels. During the 1890s Émile Levassor was constantly modifying his designs, introducing features that have become the rule. These included the enclosed gearbox (1895), the steering wheel in place of tiller (1896) and the inline four-cylinder engine (1896). Other important developments of the early days included Louis Renault's introduction of shaft drive in 1898, and the honeycomb radiator, pressed-steel frame and gate gear change of the 1901 Mercedes. The appearance of cars changed greatly as wheelbases were lengthened, and the rear-entrance tonneau gave way to the side-entrance tonneau, later to be called the touring car.

By 1904 there were several hundred firms throughout the world making automobiles, a few in numbers large enough to justify the term mass production (Oldsmobile built over 5500 that year), but many were small former bicycle makers who turned out a few indifferent and unoriginal cars each year, and soon succumbed to competition from the big battalions. The variety available to the public was very great, from such simple machines as the Orient Buckboard, which consisted of two seats on a wooden platform with a single-cylinder engine driving directly on the rear axle, to enormous luxury cars such as the 60hp Mercedes and 60hp FIAT, the latter with a capacity of over 10 litres. Even smaller than the Orient Buckboard were the tricars, which are discussed in the motorcycle section. The great majority of early cars were open, and only intended to be used in fine weather, but professional men such as doctors who had to be out in all weathers soon demanded a fixed roof over their heads, and so was born the closed coupé, often called the 'doctor's coupé' up to 1930. Once wheelbases were long enough to carry a side-entrance closed car the limousine made its appearance, with a glass partition between the chauffeur and passengers. Sometimes the chauffeur might have a roof and windscreen, and sometimes not, in which case the body style was known as a coupé de ville. A popular style was the landaulette, in which the rear portion of the body could be folded down in fine weather, a much simpler operation than removing the whole hood, as on a touring car. The landaulette style was employed on most London taxicabs up to 1939.

Steam and electric cars had passed their peak of popularity by 1910. From being simpler and cheaper than the equivalent petrol car in 1900, the steamer had become more complex and much more expensive, a 1910 Model MM White costing as much as $5000. There was still the problem of slow starting, and although pilot lights and a flash generator had reduced this to a few minutes, it was inevitably longer than one or two turns on the crank of a petrol car. White turned to petrol in 1910, leaving Stanley as the sole steam-car company catering to a dwindling market. Stanley struggled on until 1927, and was joined in the 1920s by the luxurious and extremely expensive Doble, but steam could no longer in any sense be called a significant force on the motoring scene. Unlike Britain, America never had a flourishing steam-lorry industry. The electric car was popular for its silence and ease of starting and driving, but it suffered from the same drawbacks that have so far denied commercial success to its descendants of the 1970s–limited range and low speed. It is not that an electric car cannot travel at speed; as early as 1902 a Baker covered a mile in 47sec, but such a burst of speed means that the batteries need recharging at once. You can have reasonable speed or reasonable range, but not both at the same time. In America, electric cars found a limited market for city use up to the early 1920s, after which demand became a mere trickle; nevertheless the Detroit Electric Car Company continued to offer its products up to 1938.

Shortly before the outbreak of World War I a new breed of cheap car appeared, known as the cyclecar because it shared more components with the motorcycle than with the ordinary car. The precise definition of a cyclecar, drawn up in 1912, was any car of less than 1100cc engine capacity and 772lb weight, but the expression came to be associated with two-cylinder engines, a wooden frame, and belt or chain drive. Anything with a four-cylinder engine and shaft drive, whatever its capacity, was more properly called a light car. The first cyclecars appeared in 1910, and by 1913 the boom was on, with over a hundred makes in Britain and nearly as many in America. France had fewer makes, but the Bédélia was one of the best known. In this the driver sat in tandem behind his passenger. Many cyclecars were

crude machines with uncertain steering and brakes, and negligible weather protection; and belt transmissions frequently slipped or broke. Nevertheless the better examples, such as the London-built G.N., did provide an exciting performance at a reasonable price, and this kept sales going until the arrival of the cheap four-cylinder light car in the shape of the Austin Seven and Citroën 5CV. In America cyclecars never really had a chance, for their price was only a little lower than that of a Model T Ford, which for all its defects could carry five people at up to 40mph, with spare parts available everywhere.

At the other end of the scale, makers of luxury cars were obtaining greater smoothness by increasing the number of cylinders. Up to 1903 the path to greater power was by way of enlarging the capacity of a four-cylinder engine, but there was a limit to this process which only led to roughness of running, and the logical alternative was to increase the number of cylinders to six. At first the longer crankshafts of the six-cylinder engine vibrated badly, but this was solved by the Lanchester Vibration Damper, which was a secondary flywheel at the front of the crankshaft. The six-cylinder engine was introduced by Napier in 1903, and its example was followed by a large number of manufacturers over the next few years, so that by 1912 the four-cylinder engine was a rarity in cars of over 4 litres' capacity. The next logical step was to increase the number of cylinders to eight, and this was taken by de Dion-Bouton in 1910. The cylinders were mounted in V-formation, and it was to be another ten years before the alternative layout of the straight eight appeared. Because of insufficient development the V8 de Dion was not a particularly successful car, but the design was studied by Cadillac who launched a V8 in 1914. This led to a spate of V8s in America, from such makers as Oldsmobile, Cole and King. The proprietary engine makers Herschell-Spillman added a V8 to their range in 1915, and this was used by assembled car manufacturers such as Ross. The V8 was followed by a short-lived craze for the V12, of which Packard was much the most successful exponent, making some 35,000 of its Twin Six between 1915 and 1921. Other makers, all American, who went in for the V12 included National, Hal, Shaw and Singer.

The first postwar cars to be announced in 1919 were mostly similar to prewar models, which is understandable in the light of the necessity to get cars into the showrooms, and the fact that the public were so eager to buy cars that second-hand models were selling for more than their new price in 1914. By the end of 1919, however, some striking new models had appeared that foreshadowed what the 1920s were to bring in the way of technical development. The two outstanding designs were the Hispano-Suiza H6 and the Isotta-Fraschini Tipo 8. The former was a brand-new design from a company that had originated in Spain, but whose most famous products from 1919 onwards were to come from the French factory at Bois-Colombes. It had a 6½-litre six-cylinder engine with single ohc, being one half of a projected V12 aero engine. This developed 135bhp, making it the most powerful touring car in the world, and one of the few that was equally at home in town, on the *Routes Nationales* and on the racetrack. It had four-wheel brakes which were servo operated, and unlike certain unsuccessful prewar four-wheel-brake systems, the Hispano's were coupled, operated by the footbrake only, instead of requiring simultaneous operation of hand- and footbrake. The spread of four-wheel brakes was one of the main developments of the 1920s, and by the end of the decade practically every car in the world had them. At first there was considerable suspicion among manufacturers, and those who had not yet taken up the system were loud in condemnation of it, on the grounds that it increased the risk of skidding. Their main objection, in fact, was cost, for the chassis had to be redesigned if front-wheel brakes were not hopelessly to spoil the car's handling.

The other trend-setting design, the Italian Isotta-Fraschini, also had four-wheel brakes, and in addition it boasted the world's first production eight-in-line, or straight-eight, engine. This was a logical extension of the six, but even more than this, it needed a stiff crankshaft if vibration was to be eliminated. The Isotta never quite achieved the cachet of the Hispano as its sporting successes were fewer and it had a reputation for heavy handling. It was followed by the Kenworthy and Duesenberg straight eights in America, by Leyland in Britain, and by Ballot and Bugatti in France. Gradually the straight eight spread down the scale, and the introduction by American proprietary engine builders such as Lycoming and Continental of a straight eight into their ranges meant that medium-priced assembled cars such as Jordan could boast of an eight-in-line. By 1931 60 per cent of American models had straight-eight engines, and the

type was seen in commercial vehicles and even taxicabs. The V8 seemed to be in eclipse, only to be revived in 1932 when Ford launched the first really low-priced eight-cylinder car. Even so, it was not until the early 1950s that the V8 took over from the straight eight as the standard engine for the American car. Multi-cylinderism reached its peak in the early 1930s with the V12s of Packard, Cadillac, Lincoln, Pierce-Arrow, Hispano-Suiza and others, and the V16s of Cadillac and Marmon.

The 1930s are often stigmatized as an era of dullness in car design, and of cheap mass-production methods, and although these charges can be substantiated, critics sometimes forget that many aspects of design that we take for granted today were pioneered during this much-criticized decade. Apart from the Lancia Lambda, integral construction of chassis and body was unknown in 1930, yet by 1939 it was to be found on General Motors' two European subsidiaries, Vauxhall and Opel, as well as on the American Lincoln-Zephyr, the French Citroën *traction avant* and the Italian Lancia Aprilia and Ardea. Front-wheel drive was another design that had been experimented with since the turn of the century, but was not put into mass production until the 1930s, when Citroën in France, DKW and Adler in Germany, and Aero in Czechoslovakia took up the idea. Aerodynamics were studied to a greater extent than ever before, and the results seen on such cars as the Chrysler Airflow and the rear-engined Czechoslovakian Tatra.

More important to the average motorist than radical design changes was the increased comfort and ease of driving that the 1930s brought. The synchromesh gearbox became widespread on even the cheapest cars, and easy-change systems such as the Wilson preselector and Daimler's fluid flywheel were available in the higher price ranges. In 1940 Oldsmobile introduced a genuine two-pedal automatic system with its Hydramatic drive. Other developments that made motoring more pleasant included much more widespread use of closed bodies and interior heaters. On the debit side, engines were moved further forward to give greater passenger space, which impaired handling and generally detracted from the car's appearance. This was as true of the luxury cars as of cheaper models, and few people could say that the lines of a Rolls Royce or Packard of 1939 were as handsome as those of their predecessors of ten years earlier.

The first historical display devoted to the
motor vehicle. In celebration of the 1000th
internal-combustion engine made by the
Daimler company, this collection of
machinery was assembled in the garden
attached to Gottlieb Daimler's house in the
Taubenheimstrasse, Cannstatt, on
21 December 1895. On the left in **illus. 1** is
the Stahlradwagen ('steel-wheel car') of
1889 designed by Wilhelm Maybach; on the
right is Daimler's first motorcycle of 1885.
On the stand can be seen, on the left, the
first Daimler engine, on the right the
second, and in the centre the 1000th.

2. 1891 Volk three-wheeled 1hp electric dogcart (GB)

Magnus Volk, builder of Brighton's electric seafront tramway which still operates today, made a few three-wheeled electric dogcarts in 1891. One was sold to the Sultan of Turkey—almost certainly the first export of a passenger car from Great Britain. In **illus. 2** Volk is at the tiller and his daughter is in the rear-facing seat.

France's best-known maker of electric vehicles in the 1890s was Charles Jeantaud whose products included open victorias, closed coupés, cabs, delivery vans and trucks. **Illus 3** shows a six-seater brake which he entered in the 1895 Paris-Bordeaux Race. Relays of fresh batteries were sent ahead to various points on the route, but the car retired with a broken axle soon after the start.

1. 1895 exhibition of Daimler engines and vehicles (D)

3. 1895 Jeantaud electric brake (F)

4. 1896 Benz Velo 3½hp four-seater (D)
5. 1895 Peugeot 6hp four-seater (F)

6. 1897 Daimler 6hp four-seater (GB)

9. c. 1898 Daimler four-seater (GB)

8. 1897 Daimler four-seater (GB)

Two Coventry-built Daimlers, one of 1897 (**illus. 8**) and the other (with passengers) of a year or two later (**illus. 9**). The most noticeable difference is the steering wheel on the latter in place of the tiller. This first became available in 1898, as an optional alternative to the tiller, but many older cars were subsequently re-equipped with steering wheels, so it is not a reliable dating feature for Daimlers. Frank Morriss of King's Lynn, Norfolk, official car repairer to King Edward VII, made a speciality of updating old Daimlers, rebuilding engines and gearboxes as well as altering the steering. The young man in the rear seat of the *c.* 1898 car is Warwick Wright, later to achieve fame as a driver of Minerva racing cars and as a London car retailer.

Illus. 4 is of an 1896 example of the 3½hp Benz Velo, made with little change from 1894 to 1902. Its 1045cc single-cylinder engine gave it a top speed of about 18mph, and its popularity enabled Benz to outsell all his rivals. For ten years Benz led the world in car production, and in 1896 sold more than the combined production of all the car makers in Great Britain and the United States. To many potential buyers the name Benz was synonymous with the automobile, as Ford was to become twenty years later.

Seating arrangements were very varied on nineteenth-century cars because of the problem of accommodating four passengers on a very short wheelbase. Two of the most popular solutions were the *vis-à-vis* (face to face), typified by the 1895 Peugeot (**illus. 5**) and the *dos-à-dos* (back to back) of the 1897 British-built Daimler (**illus. 6**). The Panhard (**illus. 7**) of the Hon C. S. Rolls, photographed outside his family home, The Hendre, near Monmouth, has sideways-facing seats in the style of a horse-drawn brake. Other period features shared by all three cars include tiller steering, chain drive and rear wheels larger than the front.

7. 1897 Panhard six-seater brake (F)

10. 1896 Thomson 5hp steam car (AUS)

Two of the earliest Australian cars, the Thomson steamer (**illus. 10**) and the Pioneer petrol-engined car (**illus. 11**). The Thomson was built in 1896, but it achieved its greatest fame when it was four years old, when Herbert Thomson drove it from Bathurst, N.S.W., to Melbourne, a journey of 493 miles. Many stops were made *en route* to satisfy the curiosity of press and public, so the journey took nine days, but it was still a record, and the longest journey undertaken by a horseless carriage in Australia. The photo shows the car at the Park Hotel, Bathurst, before the start, with Thomson (furthest from camera) and his partner E. L. Holmes. The Pioneer was made by the grandly named Australian Horseless Carriage Syndicate, of Melbourne, and designed by William Grayson of Fitzroy. It was demonstrated to Lord Brassey, Governor of Victoria, in February 1897, drawing favourable comment, but not more than six cars were built.

11. 1897 Pioneer four-seater *dos-à-dos* (AUS)

12. 1899 Renault 1¾hp voiturette (F)
13. 1901 Renault 3½hp voiturette (F)

Two early Renaults: Louis Renault's greatest contribution to the development of the automobile was shaft drive to a live rear axle, at a time when the bulk of front-engined cars used chain drive. Other features of his early machines, not so unusual, included a tubular frame and single-cylinder de Dion engine. His prototype of 1898 had wheel steering, but the first production model of a year later (**illus. 12**) had an unusual semi-circular tiller with hand grips at each end, and vertical column. By 1901 (**illus. 13**) wheel steering and an inclined column had been adopted. With a larger engine of 3½hp, it was felt reasonable to add an extra seat, though the leg room is minimal.

14. 1901 White steam racing car (USA)

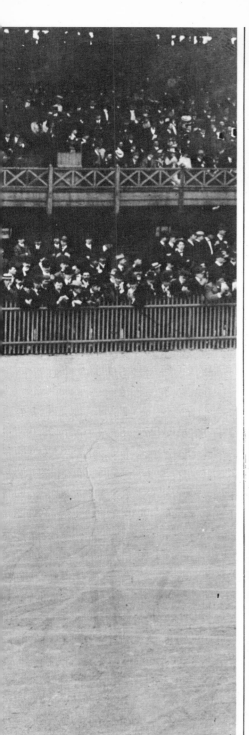

15. 1900 Winton 3·8-litre racing car (USA)

Alexander Winton was one of America's pioneer car builders. Up to 1901 he made more petrol-engined cars than any other firm, though beaten in the production league by Columbia electrics and Locomobile steamers. He was also early in the racing field, and entered this two-seater (**illus. 15**) in the first Gordon Bennett Race held in June 1900. It looked less like a racer than any of its five competitors, and retired from the fray at less than a quarter of the race's distance. The engine was an enormous single-cylinder unit of nearly 3·8 litres' capacity; later Winton built racing cars with horizontal four- and eight-cylinder engines.

17. 1905 Serpollet steam touring car (F)

16. 1902 Serpollet 'Easter Egg' steam racing car (F)

In **illus. 16** is seen a 1902 Serpollet, the best-known French steamer, at the Bexhill (Sussex) Speed Trials. This car, christened 'Easter Egg', was one of several sprint specials built by Léon Serpollet. The car in **illus. 17** is a touring model of Serpollet, dating from 1905, awaiting its turn at the Gaillon hill climb.

21

A pioneer Napier, the first four-cylinder model of 1900, built for the Paris-Toulouse-Paris Race, in which it did not distinguish itself. However, it was the prototype for a range of successful touring cars. In **illus. 18** the famous Napier protagonist S. F. Edge is at the wheel with H. L. Clark in the passenger seat, and between them Edge's dog, Don. Sad to relate, Don was killed shortly afterwards when he fell from the car at speed.

18. 1900 Napier 4·9-litre two-seater touring car (GB)

19. 1902 Lohner electric runabout (A)

A car of obscure origin, the Belle (**illus. 21**), sold by E. J. Coles of Holloway, North London. Although claimed to be of Coles's design and manufacture, it was almost certainly of Continental origin, possibly Swiss. This was a common practice when chauvinistic buyers preferred to think that their cars were genuinely British, although the really high-quality foreign cars such as Mercedes or Panhard always had a great cachet. The Belle was short lived, being made only from 1901 to 1903, but had the distinction of being the first car to be driven on the stage of a London theatre. With Coles at the wheel, it made an appearance at the Alhambra, Leicester Square, in 1901.

These two photographs show the children of E. W. Hart, a well-known importer who also built several experimental cars. The girl at the tiller in **illus. 19** is eleven-year-old Marguerite Louise Hart who regularly drove her electric runabout to school and on shopping expeditions. *The Car Illustrated* observed: 'there has been no warning finger or wild gesticulation of the "gentlemen in blue" directed against *this* young lady, nor has she a record of conviction and fine to boast of like some older and more reckless drivers'. The lad at the wheel of the four-seater (**illus. 20**), also an electric, is her fourteen-year-old brother Oscar Ernest Hart. Marguerite's car is said to have been imported into Britain from Vienna by her father, and is probably a Lohner; her brother's machine looks as if it might well have been home made. This juvenile motoring was one of the casualties of the British Motor Car Act of 1903 which fixed a minimum age limit of seventeen for driving a four-wheeled vehicle.

20. 1902 four-seater electric car (GB)

One of the most popular European cars in
the early 1900s was the single-cylinder
de Dion-Bouton. It began life in 1899 as a
four-seater *vis-à-vis* with 2¾hp engine
mounted at the rear, but in 1902 the engine
was moved to the front, and a rear-entrance
tonneau body of the type shown in **illus. 22**
was adopted, although the car was also
made as a two-seater. The engine size was
increased to 6 or 8hp but the
expanding-clutch transmission was
retained. In this gear changing was effected
by a lever on the steering column; a turn
anti-clockwise expanded the low-speed
clutch to move the car away from rest, and
a turn in the opposite direction released the
low-speed clutch and actuated the high-
speed one. This system was employed by
de Dion-Bouton until 1905, when a
conventional three-speed gearbox was
adopted, although one expanding-clutch
model remained available until 1910.

22. 1902 de Dion-Bouton 6/8hp tonneau (F)

21. 1901 'Belle' 8hp tonneau (CH?)

One of the more popular American cars was the Rambler, made from 1902 to 1913. **Illus. 23** is of a 1904 Model L with an 18hp two-cylinder engine which, despite the conventional bonnet, was located under the seat in the manner of most of the cheaper American cars of its day.

The success of the Mercedes design (see **illus. 26**) led to many European and American imitations. Among the latter was Locomobile: this company gave up its light steamers after 1903 and turned to a high-quality four-cylinder car of the type in **illus. 24**, designed by A. L. Riker. This 1905 example was owned by Theo Kearney of Kearney Park, Fresno, Cal., seen here in the rear seat. Note the elaborate picnic basket.

23. 1904 Rambler 18hp Model L tourer (USA)

24. 1905 Locomobile four-cylinder tourer (USA)

26. 1903 Mercedes 24/28hp tonneau (D)

Two of the most respected names on both sides of the Atlantic were Panhard and Mercedes. Panhard was the 'senior make', but having led design during the 1890s with such important innovations as four-cylinder engines and wheel steering, its cars were becoming somewhat old fashioned by 1903, when Mercedes was setting the pace with honeycomb radiators, all-steel frames in place of the Panhard's armoured wood frame, and gate-type gear change. The photos show a large four-cylinder Panhard (**illus. 25**) of 1902–3 with extravagant lighting equipment, and a 1903 Mercedes 24/28hp tonneau (**illus. 26**). Seated next to the driver is Wilhelm Maybach who was largely responsible for the Mercedes' design.

25. 1902-3 Panhard four-cylinder tourer (F)

27. 1902 Peugeot limousine (F)

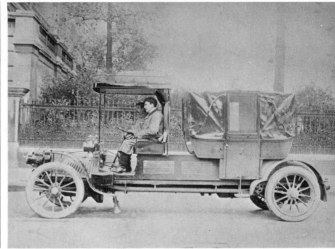

28. 1903 C.G.V. 15hp landau (F)

Closed bodies were rarely seen on the earliest cars, but as wheelbases lengthened, permitting side entrances, they became increasingly popular. The 1902 Peugeot (**illus. 27**) carries a rear-entrance limousine body by the famous Parisian coachbuilders, J. Rothschild et Fils. In contrast to the short Peugeot, the 1903 15hp C.G.V. (**illus. 28**) built for Miss Alice de Rothschild has one of the longest wheelbases of any car of its time, rather more than 12ft. It was a motorized landau for station work, and was specially low-geared in order to cope with the very steep gradients from Grasse station to the Villa Victoria, Miss de Rothschild's Riviera residence. Luggage could be carried in the lockers between the driving and passenger compartments, as well as on the roof rack. **Illus. 29** shows another French car, a 40hp Rochet-Schneider of 1906 with

29. 1906 Rochet-Schneider 40hp coupé (F)

30. 1908 Austin 18/24hp limousine (GB)

a coupé body. This style was more popular on smaller, owner-driver cars. The conventional limousine style is shown in **illus. 30**, a Barker body on a 1908 Austin. This particular body dates from 1910, and was the third to be fitted to the chassis. In two years this had covered over 25,000 miles without any mechanical defect, including a 2000-mile tour of Switzerland. Touring limousine would be the best description for the body in **illus. 31**, built on a specially lengthened 80hp six-cylinder Welch chassis for its owner, Mr Nat Goodwin. It was said to contain a sleeping berth, bath, refrigerator, crockery cabinet and other conveniences for touring'. The wheelbase was 11ft 10in and the weight 3 tons. The Welch was a high-quality American car, distinguished by pioneer use of an overhead-camshaft engine.

31. 1909 Welch 80hp touring limousine (USA)

32. 1905 Grégoire two-seater (F)

33. 1905 Clément-Bayard sprint car (F)

Two contrasting competition cars of 1905.
Illus. 32 is a Grégoire light car taking part
in the Concours des Voiturettes, a six-day
trial followed by speed events, for cars with
a maximum engine capacity of 1 litre. The
1905 event was rather a fiasco, being
hampered by appalling weather and an
unhelpful character who scattered the road
between Paris and Poissy with large bent
nails. However, it was the predecessor of
the highly successful and significant Coupe
des Voiturettes races of 1906 to 1913.
Illus. 33 shows a Clément-Bayard at the
weigh-in before a hill climb at Gaillon. In
order to reduce its weight as much as
possible, the body has been reduced to the
minimum of one seat and the chassis frame
has been liberally drilled, not only at the
sides of the channel frame, but also on top.

28

34. 1907 N.A.G. touring car (D)

35. 1907 Argyll touring car (GB)

Although racing claimed most of the glamour of early motoring competition, there were also a number of long-distance road trials for touring cars, such as the Herkomer and Prince Henry Trials in Germany, and the Critérium de France. These photos show (**illus. 34**) an N.A.G. in the 1907 Herkomer Trial, and three competitors in the Critérium de France of the same year: an Argyll (**illus. 35**), a Gladiator (**illus. 36**), and a Lorraine-Dietrich (**illus. 37**). The Scottish-built Argyll was the only British competitor in the event, which was stopped after an accident involving a competing car and a press car, in which five people were killed.

36. 1907 Gladiator touring car (F)

37. 1907 Lorraine-Dietrich touring car (F)

There was never an extensive motor industry in Tsarist Russia, but recent investigation has brought a number of makes to light, including Lessner, Puzyrev, Russo-Buire and, the best known, the Russo-Baltic made in Riga. This was produced from 1909 to 1915 in a variety of models, all with fairly large four-cylinder engines. After the 1917 Revolution, a few Russo-Baltics were assembled in Moscow (**illus. 95**). Illus. 38 shows a 24/30hp Model K tourer of 1912.

38. 1912 Russo-Baltic Model K 24/30hp tourer (SU)

39. 1910 Mercedes 75hp tourer (D)

A Barker-bodied Rolls-Royce Silver Ghost tourer of 1909 (**illus. 41**). This body style was an ancestor of the convertible sedan of the 1930s, at least as far as the passenger compartment was concerned, for it could be completely enclosed in bad weather, and the doors contained pull-up windows of the railway carriage pattern, complete with tasselled strap. Barker & Company built many bodies on Rolls-Royce chassis, although C. S. Rolls's statement in 1905 that 'all Rolls-Royce cars will be fitted with Barker bodies' did not hold good for very long.

40. 1913 Mercedes 75hp tourer (D)

Chain drive had largely been replaced by the propeller shaft, even on the largest cars, by 1910, but one firm that retained chains on its big cars was Mercedes. These photos show examples of the 75hp four-cylinder Mercedes, both with English bodies.
Illus. 39 has touring coachwork by Moss Brothers of Fulham; **illus. 40** is of a 1913 75hp chassis with a body built shortly after

World War I by Compton & Hermon, of Walton-on-Thames, to the order of Earl Cowley. The 75hp (known in Germany as the 38/70PS) had a capacity of 8950cc, and there was an even larger 90hp (37/90PS) with a capacity of 9500cc. Both of these were replaced in 1914 by the more modern, shaft-drive 28/95PS which was continued for a number of years in the 1920s.

41. 1909 Rolls-Royce Silver Ghost 40/50hp tourer (GB)

42. 1913 Vauxhall Prince Henry sports car (GB)

43. 1911 Mercer Type 35 Raceabout (USA)

The sports car, as distinct from a stripped powerful tourer or superannuated racing car, emerged on both sides of the Atlantic in about 1910, but took different forms. In Europe engine development led to greatly increased power from relatively small power units, whereas the typical American speedster used a stock touring engine in a light, lowered chassis. These photos show a Prince Henry Vauxhall of 1913 (**illus. 42**) and a 1911 Mercer 35 Raceabout (**illus. 43**). At the wheel of the latter is the famous American racing driver, Ralph DePalma, giving actress Dorothy Lane a spin on the Vanderbilt Cup circuit at Santa Monica, Cal.

44. 1912 Auto-Aéro propeller-driven car (F)

An oddity of 1912, the propeller-driven Auto-Aéro designed by Count Bertrand de Lesseps (**illus. 44**). This seems to have been very much a home-made job, but propeller-driven cars, by Leyat and Traction Aérienne, were actually offered for sale in France in the 1920s, and a German Maybach was experimentally fitted with a radial aero engine as late as 1938. Among the chief drawbacks of these cars were leisurely acceleration, absence of engine braking, and an unacceptably high noise level.

45. 1912 Wolseley Gyrocar (GB)

Another unconventional design, the
Wolseley Gyrocar of 1912 (**illus. 45**).
Designed by the Russian Count Peter
Schilowsky, it was powered by a stock
Wolseley car engine, and while on its two
wheels was kept in balance by a gyroscope
which rotated at 1500rpm and absorbed no
more than 1·25hp from the engine. When the
car came to a standstill and the engine was
stopped, the small stabilizing wheels which
can be seen in the photograph were lowered
automatically. So long as the engine was
running, and driving the gyroscope, the car
could be driven at walking speed, and even
stopped and put into reverse, without need
for the stabilizers. Schilowsky's Gyrocar
was tested at the Wolseley factory and in
London, but the war prevented any further
development.

46. 1906 Piccolo 12hp two-seater (D)

34

Development of the light car, 1906–14. Small cars followed two lines of development: the large car in miniature and the cyclecar, which owed more to motorcycle practice. **Illus. 46** is an example of the former, a German-built Piccolo of 1906 with aircooled two-cylinder engine and shaft drive; **illus. 47**, a British Phoenix of 1907, shows signs of its descent from the Phoenix Trimo tricar (**illus. 348**). Chief among these are the tubular radiators mounted on each side of the dashboard. It was powered by a horizontally mounted single- or two-cylinder engine, and final drive was by single chain. A number of the cyclecars were three-wheelers, and of these the best known was the Morgan; **illus. 48** shows a runabout of 1912. Many cyclecars used unconventional forms of transmission, such as friction drive. In this two discs engaged at right angles, the different positions of the driving disc on the face of the driven one giving varying gear ratios. The best-known British car to feature this system was the G.W.K., of which a 1913 model is shown in **illus. 49**. The two-cylinder engine was mounted behind the driver; G.W.K.s of the 1920s (**illus. 81**) had front-mounted engines. but still used friction drive.

47. 1907 Phoenix 8hp two-seater (GB)

48. 1912 Morgan 8hp runabout (GB)
49. 1913 G.W.K. two-cylinder two-seater (GB)

A true light car was the first Morris Oxford (**illus. 50**), powered by a 1018cc four-cylinder engine made by White & Poppe. It is seen here, with its designer William Morris at the wheel, before setting out for the 1913 London-Edinburgh trial. The car's first exhibition appearance was at the Manchester Motor Show in February 1913, but no demonstration runs could be made as the cylinder block and sump were made of wood! One of the best-quality light cars of the pre-1914 period was the Bugatti (**illus. 51**), at that time a German car as its home town of Molsheim was in Alsace, German territory until after 1918. Its controls were so light that vintage-car enthusiast Cecil Clutton wrote of it: 'it is essentially to be controlled with fingers and toes rather than with hands and feet. The gear lever is flicked rather than pushed or pulled.' The photo shows a Bugatti Type 13 at the start of the 1913 Coupe de la Meuse.

50. 1913 Morris Oxford two-seater (GB)

51. 1913 Bugatti Type 13 two-seater (D)

A car that rivalled the light two-seaters in price, while carrying four or five passengers with ease, was the famous Ford Model T (**illus. 52**). It was launched in October 1908 with a price tag of $850, but by 1914, the year of the model in **illus. 52**, the price was down to $490, thanks to mass production which increased the number of cars made from 100 a day in 1909 to more than 1000 a day four years later. The Model T's production peak was not reached until 1923, when 1,817,891 cars were made, and the price of the cheapest model was down to $269.

52. 1914 Ford Model T 2·9-litre tourer (USA)

53. 1913 White tourer (USA)

Bad roads were a bugbear to the early
motorist all over the world, but nowhere
more so than in the United States, where a
mile or two outside the large towns
near-medieval conditions prevailed, with
deep mud in wet weather. This large 1913
White touring car (**illus. 53**) seems firmly
wedged on a rock; as no rope is visible, the
passenger is evidently urging the driver on
rather than giving any physical assistance.

In order to cope with bad roads, a number of British firms offered 'colonial' versions of their touring cars, with greater ground clearance than on the domestic product. On this experimental Standard of 1913 (**illus. 54**) the designers have gone one better by offering four-wheel drive as well, though this was never seen on a production model. Although drive to all wheels became popular on trucks during and after World War I, it has had only very limited application to passenger cars.

A 1914 Cadillac with British landaulette body (**illus. 55**). Though by no means the most expensive American car of its day, the make pioneered a number of important features, most significant of which was the electric starter. This was introduced on the 1912 models and was a great improvement on the crude compressed-air starters that had been used hitherto, although the majority of cars were started on the crank. The Cadillac also featured electric lighting.

54. 1913 Standard Colonial tourer (GB)

55. 1914 Cadillac 20/30hp landaulette (USA)

56. 1913 Lozier tourer (USA)

One of the highest-quality American cars of the pre-1914 era was the Lozier which appealed to the same sort of market as Daimler and Delaunay-Belleville in Europe. Prices ran as high as $5000 for the chassis alone. The 1913 tourer in **illus. 56** was used for taking members of the Biograph Cinema Company on location in New York in 1915.

57. 1914 Renault enclosed limousine (F)

By 1914 the completely enclosed limousine was becoming more commonplace, although the sedanca de ville or town car with open chauffeur compartment was to remain popular for another twenty years. These two enclosed limousines show contrasting schools of styling—the opulent curves of the Renault (**illus. 57**) and the rather severe lines of the Nazzaro (**illus. 58**). The latter was an Italian car, although the body is British, by Newton & Bennett of Manchester.

58. 1914 Nazzaro 20/30hp enclosed limousine (I)

The odd little vehicle in **illus. 59** is not a taxicab, but a specially built town car designed by a New Yorker for his wife's exclusive use. The engine is at the rear, below the driver's seat, and drive is by chains to the front wheels. The cost of this one-off, made in 1910, is said to have been $7000.

The Prince Henry Trials, which had been such a formative influence on sports-car design from 1908 to 1910, became a leisurely tour of stately homes in Germany and Britain in 1911, the last year in which they were held. Here is N. C. Neill's Rolls-Royce Silver Ghost in a garden-party scene typical of the 1911 event (**illus. 60**). By contrast, in France there were several really testing road events such as the newly instituted Monte Carlo Rally and the Tour de France. **Illus. 61** shows Saumon's six-cylinder Delage saloon during the 1912 Tour de France

59. 1910 custom-built town car (USA)
60. 1911 Rolls-Royce Silver Ghost 40/50hp tourer (GB)

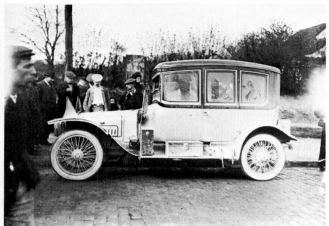

61. 1912 Delage six-cylinder saloon (F)

A motorized picnic in 1914. The early example of Vauxhall 30/98 (**illus. 62**) has sketchier running boards than many cars, but even so one is used to support the primus stove. Modern motorists do not realize what a useful adjunct to a successful picnic the traditional running board was.

62. 1913-14 Vauxhall 30/98 sporting four-seater (GB)

64. 1911-12 Vauxhall Thirty six-cylinder touring limousine (GB)

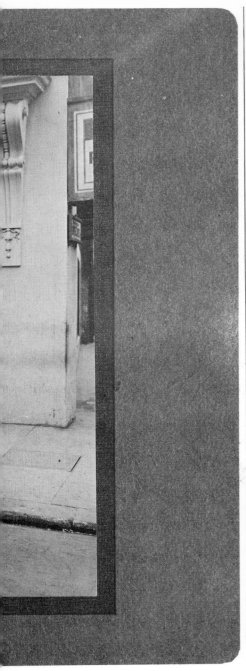

63. 1915 Jeffery dual-purpose car (USA)

Family outing in a 1915 Jeffery dual-purpose car (illus. 63). The seats behind the driver could be removed to make a light truck for delivery work during the week, while for Sunday jaunts it was a full six-seater touring car. One American concern, the Day Automobile Company of Detroit, specialized in this type of vehicle, but many firms such as Jeffery offered them as part of a wide range of cars and trucks.

65. 1911-12 Vauxhall Thirty six-cylinder tourer (GB)

The fame of Vauxhall's sporting models, the Prince Henry and the 30/98, has tended to obscure the high-quality six-cylinder touring cars which the company also made. These photos show two examples of the 1911-12 Thirty, a beautiful all-weather touring limousine (illus. 64) and a tourer built for the managing director of the Palmer Tyre Company (illus. 65). This is fitted with Palmer Cord low-pressure tyres which were a rare sight at this time. Another very unusual feature for a Vauxhall is the absence of the traditional bonnet flutes. This must have been another special request of Mr Palmer's.

43

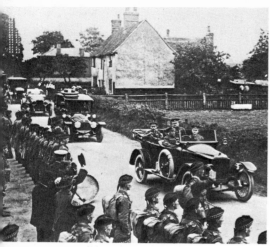

Two of the most popular makes of British Army staff car during World War I were Sunbeam and Vauxhall. Most of the former were in fact made by Rover as the Sunbeam factory was committed to aero-engine manufacture. **Illus. 66** shows a Sunbeam 16hp somewhere in northern France, with a primitive traffic signal. The Vauxhall 25hp in **illus. 67** carries King George V and General Sir Arthur Paget, reviewing a battalion of the Royal Scots. Behind the Vauxhall is a civilian-type Sunbeam limousine.

Lawrences' Garage at Brixton in South London in August 1921 (**illus. 68**). Petrol pumps, such as these Bowser units, were becoming more widespread, although in country districts fuel was still sold by the can. Note the clumsy, three-wheeled tyre-inflating machine.

67. c. 1916 Vauxhall 25hp tourer (GB)

66. c. 1915 Sunbeam 16hp tourer (GB)

68. 1921 garage in London

In the early 1920s the cyclecar flourished,
and some were even more crude and bizarre
than their prewar ancestors had been.
Among the more conventional was the
Peugeot Quadrilette (**illus. 69**), of which
3500 were made between 1920 and 1922.
They were powered by a tiny four-cylinder
engine of 667cc, and the original models,
such as the one illustrated, had tandem
seating. Later, the seats were staggered, but
were still more in tandem than in
side-by-side layout. The Quadrilette had
shaft drive to a worm-drive rear axle
without differential, and lighting was by
acetylene on early models. It was also
offered as a light van or single-passenger
taxicab. One of the more popular British
contemporaries of the Peugeot was the
Grahame-White, of which a batch is seen
outside the Hendon, North London, factory
in 1920 (**illus. 70**). This had a 7hp V-twin
engine and friction transmission. The
Grahame-White company also made
coachwork for expensive cars such as
Rolls-Royce, and domestic and office
furniture.

69. 1920 Peugeot Quadrilette 667cc cyclecar (F)

70. 1920 Grahame-White 7hp cyclecars (GB)

71. 1924 Scott Sociable 578cc cyclecar (GB)

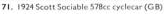

73. 1923 Mauser Einspurauto 510cc cyclecar (D)

72. 1920-2 A.V. Monocar (GB)

74. 1920 Cambro 192cc cyclecars (GB)

One of the simplest vehicles on the British market was the A.V. Monocar (**illus. 72**), strictly a single-seater with no weather protection whatsoever. Steering was by the outmoded centre-pivot system, in which the whole axle turned with the wheels. Three different engine sizes were available, 654cc, 771cc and 965cc. **Illus. 73** might almost find itself in the motorcycle section, were it not for its all-enveloping coachwork, car-type radiator and small stabilizing wheels, for it is basically a two-wheeler. It is a Mauser Einspurauto, made from 1923 to 1927 by the famous German armaments works, and also built in France under the name Monotrace. A 510cc single-cylinder engine gave it a maximum

speed of 50mph. The Scott Sociable (**illus. 71**) was an unusual three-wheeler with a triangulated tubular frame and a wheel at each corner of the triangle. It was powered by a 578cc two-cylinder two-stroke engine as used in Alfred Angas Scott's motorcycles, which were much better known than his car.

Despite their child's pedal car appearance, the three Cambro cyclecars in **illus. 74** were intended for adult use, being advertised as the cheapest cars in the world, which they probably were at 79 guineas (£82.95). The engine had a capacity of 192cc, and only one speed was provided. Fuel consumption of 100mpg was claimed.

The A.B.C. was a popular British light car of the 1920s, and like many others was made in sports form, with polished aluminium body and pointed tail, and disc wheels in place of the artillery type seen on the touring models. The standard A.B.C. had a 1203cc flat-twin engine developing 24bhp, but the 1925 Super Sports in **illus. 75** had a larger engine of 1320cc and 40bhp. Maximum speed was not far short of 70mph.

With a radiator like a miniature Rolls-Royce, the Windsor was a high-quality small car made for only three years, 1924 to 1927, just off Ladbroke Grove in London's North Kensington district by James Bartle & Co. Unlike many of its contemporaries, the company did not buy engines from outside; the 1353cc overhead-valve four-cylinder unit was its own manufacture and gave a top speed of over 60mph on the sports model shown (**illus. 77**). All Windsors had four-wheel brakes, and body styles ranged from sports cars to a sedanca de ville. The high price inseparable from quality and small-scale production prevented the Windsor from being a great success, but the firm continued in business as general ironfounders, and its name can be seen today on many of London's manhole covers.

75. 1925 A.B.C. Super Sports 12/40hp two-seater (GB)

76. 1922 Bob 1½-litre sports car (D)

In Germany as in Britain, most light-car makers offered a sports model. This is a 1½-litre Bob (**illus. 76**) which differed from the touring model in having not only a larger engine but an underslung chassis as well. Only two of these were made. Seated in the car is Zora Arkus-Duntov who was later to achieve fame for his development work on the Chevrolet Corvette.

Three light cars taken during the 1922 Scottish Six Days Trial (**illus. 78**): a 10hp Vulcan, 6CV Mathis and Salmson AL sports, in rugged Highland country. Organized for cars of between 750cc and 1600cc, this trial covered a total of 1020 miles and included several severe hills such as the celebrated 'Rest and Be Thankful'. Forty-four cars took part; there was no overall winner, but among those makes that did well in their classes were Stoneleigh, Amilcar, Talbot, Star and Riley.

77. 1926 Windsor 10/15hp sports car (GB)

78. 1922 Vulcan 10hp (GB), Mathis 6CV (F) and Salmson AL sports (F)

A selection of British light cars in rural settings. **Illus. 79** shows a 1920 10hp Deemster by the 18th green on the Worthing golf course, during an *Autocar* road test. The 1086cc Deemster was a well-made light car, and the testers' only criticism was of the jerky suspension. A rival to the Deemster was the 10hp Calcott, seen in **illus. 80** by the River Thames at Runnymede.

79. 1920 Deemster 10hp light car (GB)

80. 1922 Calcott 10hp light car (GB)

81. 1920 G.W.K. 10hp light car (GB)

Illus. 81 depicts a 10hp G.W.K. of 1920. This car retained the friction transmission of the prewar models, but in other ways it was more conventional, with a front-mounted four-cylinder engine made by Coventry-Simplex. Sales of all these cars were severely hit by the mass production and consequent price cutting of William Morris, two of whose cars are shown in **illus. 82** and **83**. The former is a Cowley sports of 1919, with special polished mahogany body made by Hollick & Pratt of Coventry. This was a one-off used by Morris himself in a number of trials of the period, but the company also made 107 sports Cowleys with aluminium bodies in 1921 and 1922. **Illus. 83** shows a Morris Oxford 14/28 with standard tourer body. The Oxford had a larger engine than the Cowley, 1802cc compared with 1550cc, and a slightly longer wheelbase.

82. 1919 Morris Cowley sports car (GB)

83. 1923 Morris Oxford 14/28hp tourer (GB)

84. 1928 Austin Seven Gordon England Cup sports car (GB)

Just as the success of Morris spelled doom to rivals such as Deemster, Calcott and Clyno, so the Austin Seven eliminated many of the under-1-litre cars. **Illus. 84** is a sports Seven known as the Gordon England Cup model, easily identifiable by its bulbous tail which contained the spare wheel. This was popular for trials such as the J.C.C. half-day trial in which this one is competing, but for racing Gordon England supplied the Brooklands Super Sports with a much higher performance.

Hill climbs on public roads continued to flourish in Britain until March 1925, when a spectator was injured at Kop Hill in Buckinghamshire. **Illus. 85** shows Raymond Mays, one of the leading hill-climb exponents, in his Brescia Bugatti on Spread Eagle Hill, near Shaftesbury, Dorset, in 1924. The record for the hill was broken no fewer than seven times on the one day, by such drivers as Malcolm Campbell (Sunbeam) and J. A. Joyce (A.C.), and was finally taken by Mays with a time of 38·6sec.

86. 1926 Frazer Nash sports car (GB)

Trials organized by local motor clubs provided a great deal of enjoyable sport for amateurs throughout the 1920s and 1930s, and did not demand the specialized vehicles that came into vogue after World War II. Anything up to 200 or 300 vehicles might take part, ordinary tourers and saloons as well as sports cars. In **illus. 86** a Frazer Nash leaves a control in the 1929 Brighton & Hove Motor Club Bognor Trial.

85. 1924 Bugatti Brescia sports car (F)

Speed hill climbs were popular throughout Europe, nowhere more than in Czechoslovakia, where the best-known hills were Zbraslav-Jíloviště, near Prague, Brno-Soběšice, and Ecce Homo. These photos show (**illus. 88**) a large 5-litre Gräf & Stift driven by F. V. Zsolnay before the start at the 1925 Ecce Homo event, and (**illus. 87**) a supercharged two-stroke six-cylinder Z on the starting line at Zbraslav-Jíloviště in May 1930. These opposed-piston two-stroke Z cars, made by the armaments firm Československá Zbrojovka, were among the most remarkable competition cars of their day and took many class victories in races and hill climbs. The Z2 illustrated developed over 60bhp from 1100cc.

87. 1929 Z2 1100cc racing car (CS)
88. 1925 Gräf & Stift 5-litre sports car (A)

One of the most important developments of the 1920s was the growth in popularity of the closed car. At the beginning of the decade the typical closed car was still the chauffeur-driven limousine, although in the United States Dodge, Essex and Ford were all offering sedans. They were, however, considerably more expensive than open tourers and consequently commanded a relatively small part of the market. Sales of closed cars overtook those of open ones in the United States in 1925; in Great Britain they represented 46 per cent of registrations in 1927, and $92\frac{1}{2}$ per cent by 1931. Typical of the boxy appearance of early 1920s saloons are the Swedish Scania-Vabis (**illus. 89**), the Czechoslovakian Walter W1Z1 (**illus. 90**) and American Essex Four Coach (**illus. 91**). The mass-produced saloon was introduced to Europe by André Citroën who began making all-steel saloons under American Budd patents in 1925. **Illus. 92** shows a Citroën B14 saloon of 1927.

89. 1920 Scania-Vabis saloon (S)

90. 1923 Walter W1Z1 25hp saloon (CS)

91. 1922 Essex Four Coach (USA)
92. 1927 Citroën B14 saloon (F)

A popular body design in the late 1920s was that patented by the Frenchman Charles T. Weymann. This had a wooden frame covered by fabric, which was in itself not unusual, but in the Weymann system the wooden members did not touch directly, being jointed by light metal strips. This eliminated the squeaking to which normal wooden frames were subject. **Illus. 93** shows a 1929 Daimler Double Six 30hp with Weymann coupé body; in **illus. 94** is seen a 1930 Stutz Vertical Eight sedan before the fitting of the leathercloth covering to the Weymann frame. Weymann bodies were used on the Stutz sports cars that raced at Le Mans, as well as on many touring Stutzes.

93. 1929 Daimler Double Six 30hp coupé (GB)

95. 1922 Russo-Baltic tourer (SU)

A very rare photo (**illus. 95**) of what is almost certainly the first car to be built in the Soviet Union after the Revolution. It is one of the small batch of Russo-Baltics made in Moscow in 1922 and has rather German lines. The front bumper is an advanced feature for the period. The next Soviet passenger car was the NAMI-1 of 1927, but serious production did not get under way until the introduction of the Ford-based GAZ-A of 1932.

The shortage of new cars in the immediate postwar period, and the availability of cheap second-hand aero engines, led to a brief vogue among enthusiasts for building their own hybrids, powered by such units as the 275bhp V12 Rolls-Royce Falcon, the 225bhp V12 Sunbeam and the 300bhp six-cylinder Maybach. The best-known of these cars were the 'Chitty-Bang-Bangs' built by Count Louis Zborowski, but among others was Colonel G. H. Henderson's Napier-Rolls-Royce, powered by a 14-litre Falcon engine in an old Napier chassis (**illus. 96**). It is seen here in 1921 on a typical French road between Le Havre and Le Mans. With the engine turning comparatively slowly you could cruise at 50–60mph, and anything near full throttle led to clutch slip, so it was impossible to establish the car's potential maximum speed.

96. 1921 Napier-Rolls-Royce tourer (GB)

97. 1923 Leyland Eight 7·3-litre Grose saloon (GB)

Beardmore Motors of Paisley were among the better-known Scottish makers of the 1920s and built some successful medium-sized sports cars, one of which took the record for Shelsley Walsh hill climb in 1925. They also ventured briefly into the large-car market with the 4-litre Thirty, shown here in two-seater form (**illus. 98**). At a chassis price of £1095, very few were sold

Another rare British luxury car, of considerably more technical interest than the Beardmore, was the Leyland Eight, with 7·3-litre straight-eight overhead-camshaft engine designed by J. G. Parry Thomas. Other features included vacuum-servo brakes and torsion-bar rear springs. When originally shown at Olympia in 1920 its chassis price of £2500 made it Britain's most expensive car, though the price was later lowered to £1875. Only eighteen of these magnificent cars were made; **illus. 97** shows a late model, of 1923, with an unusual Grose saloon body.

98. 1920 Beardmore Thirty 4-litre two-seater (GB)

Despite the challenge of firms like Leyland and Napier, the position of Rolls-Royce as Britain's leading luxury-car maker was consolidated during the 1920s. Few modifications were made to the prewar Silver Ghost design, the most important being the long-overdue adoption of four-wheel brakes in 1924. **Illus. 99** shows a Silver Ghost with limousine body by Grahame-White. Note the fitted trunks with their special compartment behind the body.

In 1922 the Rolls-Royce company abandoned its one-model policy and introduced a smaller car of 3127cc known as the Twenty. It broke with traditional practice in several ways, notably in the adoption of a central gear change and three-speed gearbox, which led J. T. C. Moore-Brabazon to describe it as 'a very excellent vehicle of somewhat uninteresting American type'. He might have been more impressed if the design had incorporated the twin overhead camshafts of the prototype engine. However, it proved too difficult to obtain the necessary silence from this layout, and production Twenties had pushrod-operated overhead valves. In 1925 four speeds and right-hand change were adopted, and the model remained in production until 1929. **Illus. 100** shows a Hooper limousine body on a 1926 chassis.

99. 1922 Rolls-Royce Silver Ghost limousine (GB)
100. 1926 Rolls-Royce Twenty limousine (GB)

101. 1922 Bentley 3-litre tourer (GB)

The 3-litre Bentley was announced in May 1919, but no car was running until December of that year and it was not until September 1921 that one was actually sold to the public. However, racing successes soon came to the new *marque*, and by the mid-1920s it was the best-known British sports car, with an aura of glamour that has survived to the present day. The 3-litre was available in three chassis lengths, and almost every conceivable body style was built, from the starkest of two-seaters to limousines. It was as a four-seater tourer that it was best known, however, and all the make's Le Mans victories were achieved with bodies of this type. **Illus. 101** shows a 1922 tourer taking part in a Vintage Sports Car Club Nidderdale (Yorkshire) Trial in 1950.

In many ways the French Hispano-Suiza combined the qualities of the Rolls-Royce and Bentley, for it was a luxury touring and town car of the greatest refinement which also competed successfully in races such as the Targa Florio and Coupe Boillot at Boulogne. It appeared in 1919 with a 6½-litre single-overhead-camshaft six-cylinder engine, known as the H6, or 37·2hp in England, and this was supplemented by an 8-litre version, the H6C (45hp) in 1924. These were continued until 1934, by which time the top car of the Hispano range was a 9·4-litre V12. The photos show (**illus. 102**) an H6C with Weymann sports touring body owned by the Marquess of Cholmondeley in 1926, and (**illus. 103**) a 1928 H6C with two-seater Compton body.

The 6½-litre Hispano-Suiza was made under licence in Czechoslovakia from 1922 to 1927, using Czech-built bodies. The manufacturer was Škoda, the famous armanents firm. Škoda also made cars of its own design as well as British Sentinel steam lorries under licence. **Illus. 104** shows a 1925 Škoda-Hispano-Suiza limousine used by the Czech President Thomas Masaryk.

102. 1926 Hispano-Suiza H6C sports tourer (F)

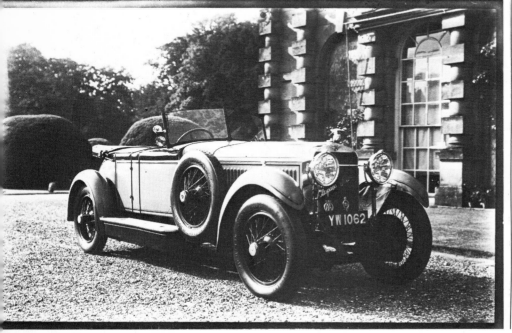

103. 1928 Hispano-Suiza H6C two-seater (F)
104. 1925 Škoda-Hispano-Suiza 6½-litre limousine (CS)

105. 1925 Voisin Model C5 4-litre tourer (F)

106. 1929 Mercedes-Benz Type SS 7-litre four-seater sports (D)

Reminiscent of the Bentley in appearance was the Voisin, product of the highly individualistic former aircraft designer Gabriel Voisin. His first car of 1919 was originally intended to be a large Citroën, and had a four-cylinder 4-litre sleeve-valve engine. It was made until 1926, when it was replaced by a range of six-cylinder cars. The best-known American enthusiast for Voisins was movie star Rudolph Valentino, seen in illus. 105 at the wheel of his 1925 Model C5 4-litre tourer.

After the fusion of the Mercedes and Benz companies in 1926, the top line of the new company was a continuation of the large six-cylinder supercharged Mercedes designed by Ferdinand Porsche. These were progressively developed through the Type K 6·2-litre, Type S 6·8-litre and the 7-litre Types SS, SSK, and SSKL, the last a sports/racing car of which only five were made. The Type S, known in England as the 36/220, was perhaps the best looking of the series, having a lower bonnet line and less

aggressive appearance than its successors. The car shown in illus. 106 is a 1929 Type SS with four-seater coachwork, owned, like the Hispano-Suiza in illus. 102, by the Marquess of Cholmondeley.

The 1920s were the heyday of the Model T Ford, and although it was an ageing design, production built up steadily from a wartime low of 436,000 in 1918 to a peak of 1,817,891 in 1923. Changes were minimal in this period, although the old joke about the T being available in any colour so long as it was black ceased to apply after 1925, when a choice of colours again appeared. Balloon tyres were introduced in 1925, and wire wheels were optional in 1926 and 1927. However, rivals such as Chevrolet were catching up, with sales nearly half those of Ford in 1926, whereas two years before Ford had outsold Chevrolet by six to one. Everyone except Henry Ford himself realized that the T would have to go, and finally in June 1927 the last 'Tin Lizzie' left the factory. **Illus. 107** shows a 1919 model with British body by the Bristol Wagon & Carriage Works; and **illus. 108** a 1927 Tudor sedan, with wire wheels and the nickel-plated radiator that characterized the last models.

108. 1927 Ford Model T Tudor sedan (USA)
107. 1919 Ford Model T landaulette (USA)

COACH WORK BY THE BRISTOL WAGON & CARRIAGE WORKS C° L.D.

109. 1928-9 Ford Model As in a showroom (USA)

Ford plants were shut down for six months during the changeover from Model T to Model A, and when the latter appeared it was something of an anti-climax. The T's epicyclic transmission had been replaced by a conventional three-speed gearbox; four-wheel brakes had come at last, but the A's appearance was still rather short and boxy for the period, and despite rumours, and actual development work on a radical X8 engine, the power unit turned out to be a conventional sv four. However, the A was never planned as more than an interim model, and although the X8 never saw the light of day, a brand-new car did appear in 1932 in the shape of the V8. The Model A had a good performance for its price ($460 for a 1929 phaeton), and sold over 3,800,000 units in five years. Among innovations of the Model A range was the first large-scale manufacture of a station-wagon body, this being introduced in 1929. A showroom display of Model As in 1928 or 1929 can be seen in **illus. 109**; **illus. 110** is a 1929 cabriolet with non-standard Woodlite headlights usually seen on much more expensive cars such as Jordan and Kissel.

110. 1929 Ford Model A cabriolet (USA)

111. 1926 Chevrolet Superior sedan (USA)

112. 1921 Essex Four tourer (USA)

The make that had been creeping up on Ford throughout the 1920s was Chevrolet, which had been acquired by General Motors in 1917. Like Ford, Chevrolet clung to a four-cylinder, rear-wheel-braked design until 1927, but in 1928 a front-wheel-braked six was introduced whose engine was not changed greatly for twenty-five years. The 1926 Superior sedan in **illus. 111** had a Fisher body with Duco cellulose finish.

Another contender in the low-price stakes was the Essex, introduced by the Hudson Motor Company of Detroit in 1919. The name is said to have emerged from the study of a map of England by Hudson executives; they almost chose Kent, but plumped for Essex on the grounds that it implied a six-cylinder engine, which in fact the car did not have, and was not to have for another six years! The original Essex engine was an inlet-over-exhaust four of 2·9 litres' capacity, developing 55bhp and giving a top speed of 60mph – considerably more than the contemporary Ford or Chevrolet. The 1921 tourer in **illus. 112** was photographed on the Berkshire Ridgeway, an ancient trackway running across southern England, and still identical in appearance and surface today.

113. 1925 Studebaker two-seater roadster (USA)

Mid-1920s fashions in clothes and car design are shown in these photos of a 1925 Studebaker (**illus. 113**) and a 1923 Dort Four (**illus. 114**). The Dort is the more conventional, having a fully enclosed two-seater coupé body of the type known in prewar days as the 'doctor's coupé', and which survived, sometimes under the name 'business coupé', well into the 1950s. Made in Flint, Mich., by former carriage builder Joshua Dallas Dort, the cars had four-cylinder Lycoming engines. The Studebaker seems at first sight to be a roadster, but though it has no sidescreens, the top is fixed. This was known as the 'California Top' and was available on two- and four-seater Studebakers from 1924 to 1927.

114. 1923 Dort Four two-seater coupé (USA)

Another example of the California Top, on a four-seater Chandler 'Chummy Roadster' of about 1923 (**illus. 115**). Although it may have had a more sporty appearance than the conventional tourer, the 'Chummy Roadster' afforded much less leg room for rear-seat passengers. In most respects the Chandler was a conventional medium-sized and priced car, using its own make of six-cylinder engine. Wire wheels were an optional extra, but made for a more handsome-looking car.

The Cleveland (**illus. 116**) was made by a Chandler subsidiary. The Chandler company wanted to widen its range and coverage of the market without cheapening the image of its own name. The Cleveland had a considerably smaller engine of 3·3 litres' capacity and cost $995 for a touring car, which in the Chandler range was priced at $1785. Note the cycle-type wings and step plates instead of running boards, a popular styling feature of American cars in the mid-1920s.

One of the many conventional 1920s American cars in the middle price range was the Stephens Salient Six (**illus. 117**), made originally by a subsidiary of the Moline Plow Company. Although they had handsome rounded radiators, most Stephens cars were rather staid in appearance, with artillery wheels. A few more dashing models were made, such as the 1923 roadster illustrated, with wire wheels and step plates. The Stephens slogan was 'Tis a Great Car'.

Easily mistaken for a Rolls-Royce, the Roamer from Kalamazoo, Mich., was an assembled car that used a variety of engines during its fourteen-year life from 1916 to 1930. These included Continental, Rochester-Duesenberg and Rutenber. Of these, the Rochester-Duesenberg gave the highest performance, some 85bhp from 5½ litres. But despite this, and the Roamer's aristocratic appearance, it did not really have any great individuality, and sales dropped from a peak of 1650 in 1920 to fewer than 500 per year from 1923 onwards. The photos show a 1921 tourer in an obviously posed shot at a naval training station (**illus. 118**) and a stripped roadster of about 1923 (**illus. 119**). Note the sign 'Tables for Ladies' above the restaurant window.

115. c. 1923 Chandler 'Chummy Roadster' (USA)

116. 1924-5 Cleveland 3·3-litre roadster (USA)

117. 1923 Stephens Salient Six 25hp roadster (USA)
119. c. 1923 Roamer 5-litre stripped roadster (USA)

118. 1921 Roamer 5-litre tourer (USA)

Captain Eddie Rickenbacker had already achieved fame as a racing driver and become a national hero for his air exploits during World War I, before he set up as a car manufacturer in 1922. The car was originally to have been called the American Ace, but it was decided that the captain's name was as good a selling point as any, and it went onto the market as the Rickenbacker. The engine was a small six of 3·6 litres, and a feature was the use of two flywheels, one at each end of the crankshaft, a similar principle to Frederick Lanchester's torsional vibration damper of 1909. Another feature of the Rickenbacker was its front-wheel brakes, introduced in June 1923, the first time these had been seen on a reasonably priced American car. **Illus. 120** shows a 1925 model.

The most significant new make of car in America in the 1920s was the Chrysler, launched at the end of 1924 by Walter P. Chrysler who had previously worked wonders with the reorganization of Willys, and had then bought Maxwell. The first Chrysler 70 was remarkable for the power (70bhp) developed by its small six-cylinder engine of 3·3 litres, and for its hydraulic four-wheel brakes. The roadster was a popular Chrysler body style from the start; **illus. 121** shows a 77 roadster of 1930.

120. 1925 Rickenbacker 3·6-litre sedan (USA)
121. 1930 Chrysler 77 roadster (USA)

The 1920s saw a great mortality rate among American car makers, even before the Depression of 1929 onwards. Most of the less distinguished assembled cars had gone before 1925, but two makes with sound reputations and reasonable annual productions that foundered at the end of the decade were Chandler and Moon. Both had ventured into the already overcrowded field of the straight-eight engine. Chandler was absorbed by Hupmobile in 1929, and Moon became involved with New Era Motors and Kissel in an attempt to manufacture the front-wheel-drive Ruxton, a merger that soon killed off all three makes. The photos show a 1927 Moon Aerotype Eight sedan on one of San Francisco's switchback streets (**illus. 122**) and a 1928 Chandler coupé, probably also taken in San Francisco (**illus. 123**).

122. 1927 Moon Aerotype Eight sedan (USA)
123. 1928 Chandler 33hp coupé (USA)

The Dorris from St Louis, Mo., was a high-quality, small-production car that used its own make of 6·2-litre six-cylinder overhead-valve engine. In 1921 about 1000 cars had been sold, but by 1923 production was barely a tenth of that figure and manufacture ceased early the following year. The Dorris slogan was 'Built up to a Standard, not down to a Price', and the cost of the 1923 Pasadena Phaeton shown (**illus. 124**) was $4150.

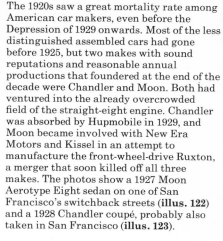

124. 1923 Dorris Pasadena Phaeton (USA)

125. 1920 Cadillac V8 town car (USA)

Cadillac was not the symbol of wealth and success that it was to become later, but was always a respected name. Nevertheless, custom bodybuilders sometimes tried to disguise the Cad's origins, an example being the cars of Inglis Uppercu which looked like Rolls-Royces. The 1920

Cadillac in **illus. 125** is not so heavily disguised, but carries an unusual town-car body. Interesting features are the carriage lamps ahead of the rear doors, unusual running board to the rear doors, and Grüss air springs behind the bumpers.

126. 1919 Daniels in a showroom (USA)

The Daniels was another high-quality car made in small numbers, although its fortunes were much less secure than, for example, the Cunningham manufactured until 1935, and production lasted only from 1916 to 1924. A wide range of bodies was offered, from the town car, coupé and touring models seen in this 1919 New York

Show photograph **(illus. 126)**, to the two-seater Submarine Speedster, one of that race of impractical but exciting cars that were so popular among the country-club set. The Daniels carried no nameplate, and its only identification was the letter 'D' embossed on the hubcaps.

127. 1923-4 Locomobile 48s (USA)

Another New York Show shot, this time of the Locomobile stand in about 1923. With its slogan 'An Exclusive Car for Exclusive People', the Locomobile was about the most expensive car on the market, apart from the American Rolls-Royce and some imported cars. Prices ran up to $13,000, for which the customer received a car of the highest quality but old-fashioned design, with T-head six-cylinder engine. Front-wheel brakes were optional; of the cars shown in **illus. 127** the sedan has them but the touring has not. The Locomobile 48 was joined in 1925 by a much cheaper car in the Buick class, the Junior Eight.

One of the most advanced American cars of its time was the Duesenberg, designed by the Duesenberg brothers who had been building successful racing cars since 1912. Their first road-going car was the Model A, launched in 1920. Two important 'firsts' stand to its credit, the first straight-eight engine fitted to a production American car, and the first use of hydraulically operated front-wheel brakes. About 600 were made between 1921 and 1927, the last year's production being loosely known as Model X, after E. L. Cord had taken over the company. **Illus. 128** shows a limousine of 1925.

A group of Pierce-Arrow sixes in a garage, *c.* 1928 (**illus. 129**). This was the last year of six-cylinder Pierce-Arrows, and henceforth the company would build only eights and twelves. Artillery wheels, as worn by the coupé and sedan on the right, were still available, though most customers preferred to pay a little extra for wire wheels. (The sedan is a few years older than the other cars.)

128. 1925 Duesenberg Model A 4·2-litre limousine (USA)

129. *c.* 1928 Pierce-Arrow sixes (USA)

The American Rolls-Royce company was approaching the end of its days in 1929 when this Brewster-bodied Phantom I York roadster was made (**illus. 130**). A total of 2944 American Rolls-Royces were made between 1921 and 1931, and although the Depression is often blamed for the closure of the Springfield plant, it is doubtful if the Phantom II, introduced in Britain in 1930, would ever have gone into production in the United States: retooling costs would have been very high, and Rolls of America was meeting increasing competition from Cadillac, Packard, Lincoln and Marmon, all of whom were offering more cylinders – eights, twelves, and the Cadillac and Marmon V16s – at lower prices.

130. 1929 Rolls-Royce Phantom I roadster (USA)

131. c. 1918 Stutz Bearcat speedster (USA)

The American speedster of the 1910s and 1920s was a fascinating phenomenon in that many of the breed were extremely handsome and sporty looking, 'made to look fast even when they were standing still' someone said of them, but their performance and handling did not necessarily match up to their appearance. One of the reasons for this was that there were no competitions for sports cars in America at this time, and not until the late 1920s did American cars appear in Europe for events such as Le Mans. With its negligible luggage accommodation and limited weather protection, the speedster was hardly ever used for long-distance touring and was mostly bought as a second car by wealthy customers who might do their day-to-day travelling in a chauffeur-driven Locomobile or Pierce-Arrow. The speedster was ideal for short runs to the increasingly popular and prestigious country clubs, yacht clubs or polo grounds.

Illus. 131 and **132** show the two best-known speedsters, the Stutz Bearcat and Mercer 22/70 Raceabout dating from 1918 and 1916 respectively. Both had large, relatively slow-turning four-cylinder engines, though the Stutz could be had with a six as well.

132. c. 1916 Mercer 22/70 Raceabout (USA)

73

134. 1921 Haynes speedster (USA)

Illus. 133 is a picture of a much rarer
speedster, the New York City-built Noma
which was powered by six-cylinder engines
made by either Continental or Beaver. The
car is shown on test in England, where it
was hoped an assembly plant would be set
up, but nothing came of this and Noma was
out of business by the end of 1923. Haynes,
whose speedster is shown in **illus. 134**, was
an old-established company most of whose
products were staid-looking touring cars or
sedans. The wire-wheeled speedster was a
new model for 1921 and could be had with a
six- or twelve-cylinder engine. One of the
best-looking of the speedsters was the
Paige-Daytona **(illus. 135)** built by the
Paige-Detroit Motor Car Company and
named in honour of the 102·83mph record
established by a stock Paige in 1921. The
Daytona had a 5·4-litre six-cylinder
Continental engine which gave it a top
speed of 80mph. It was a two-seater, but an
additional passenger could be carried on a
third seat which could be pulled out like a
drawer from the side of the body. The photo
shows a 1922 model; in 1923 front and rear
bumpers and side-mounted spare wheels
were added. Only fifty-six Daytona
roadsters were made.

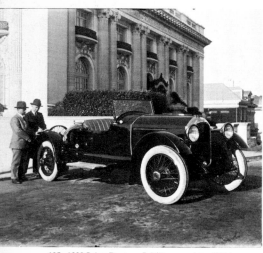

135. 1922 Paige-Daytona 5·4-litre speedster (USA

133. 1921 Noma Six 27hp speedster (USA)

Introduced in 1931, the Mercedes-Benz 170 (**illus. 137**) was the first move by the famous German company into the small popular car market. It had a six-cylinder engine of 1692cc which developed only 32bhp. giving it an uninspiring maximum speed of 55mph, but among its features not found on contemporary British cars was all-independent suspension, by twin transverse springs at the front, and twin coils and swing axles at the rear. It was made from 1931 to 1935 when it was replaced by another 170, the four-cylinder 170V of almost identical capacity.

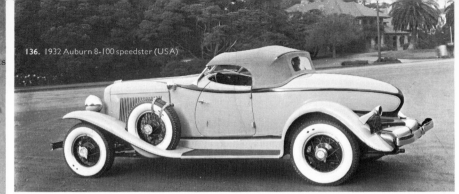

136. 1932 Auburn 8-100 speedster (USA)

137. 1931 Mercedes-Benz 170 six-cylinder saloon (D)

138. 1931 Trojan RE 1488cc saloon (GB)

A deviation from the prevailing conventionality of British cars of the 1930s was provided by the rear-engined Trojan RE saloon (**illus. 138**). This used the same 1488cc two-stroke engine as the mid-engined, solid-tyred Trojan of the 1920s, mounted vertically in the boot of what was otherwise quite a modern-looking two-door saloon. Unfortunately a top speed of only 45mph did not seem very good value for a price of nearly £180, with an electric starter extra and only two-wheel brakes. Fewer than 200 were sold in 1931-35.

The speedster was all but dead by 1925, but there was a brief revival a few years later when one of the leading lights was the Auburn, which had been transformed from one of America's most humdrum cars to one of the best looking after E. L. Cord's takeover in 1924. **Illus. 136** shows an 8-100 speedster of 1932, powered by a six-cylinder Lycoming engine and costing only $1395. A V12 engine was also available in a generally similar-looking car.

Up to 1935 the three-wheeled car was considered a motorcycle for taxation purposes in Britain: the owner paid only £4.00 compared with a sliding-scale horsepower tax for four-wheelers. Thus quite a number of three-wheelers flourished in the early 1930s, particularly B.S.A. and Morgan. The B.S.A. was almost unique among British cars in having front-wheel drive and was made in both two- and four-cylinder form. **Illus. 139** shows a 1934 four-cylinder model taking part in the Motor Cycling Club's Land's End Trial. The Raleigh Safety Seven (**illus. 140**) was unusual in having a single front wheel, but this had the advantage of allowing for a reasonably roomy four-seater body to be fitted. A saloon was made as well as this tourer, and over 3000 Raleighs were produced in four years.

139. 1934 B.S.A. four-cylinder three-wheeler (GB)

140. 1934 Raleigh Safety Seven three-wheeler (GB)

141. 1936 Lloyd 350cc two-seater (GB)

One of the very few really small four-wheelers made in Britain in this period was the Lloyd 350 produced in the fishing port of Grimsby, Lincolnshire. It had a rear-mounted two-stroke engine of 350cc, four-wheel independent suspension, and cost only £75. **Illus. 141** shows one of the fleet of Lloyds used by the Gas Light & Coke Company for its inspectors.

One of several makes of German minicar, the 494cc two-stroke Standard Superior (**illus. 142**) was of greater technical interest than most, with its tubular-backbone frame and transverse semi-elliptic spring independent suspension. It was designed by the inventive Josef Ganz who built many light-car prototypes as well as editing the lively magazine, *Motor Kritik*. Ganz had no factory, and the cars were built in the works of Wilhelm Gutbrod who made cars under his own name in the 1950s.

142. 1933 Standard Superior 494cc saloon (D)

Another Ganz design, built in Switzerland in 1938. This attractive-looking two-seater (**illus. 143**) had a rear-mounted single-cylinder opposed-piston M.A.G. engine of 350cc capacity. Several prototypes were tested during the war, and in 1946 it was put into production by the motor-scythe firm, Rapid Motormäher AG of Zürich. It was a financial disaster for the firm, however, and only thirty-six cars were made.

143. 1938 Erfiag 350cc two-seater (CH)

144. 1932 Ford V8 Model 18 3·6-litre modified roadster (USA)

The Ford V8 was one of the most significant American cars of the 1930s, introducing the V8 engine to the mass market for the first time (Chevrolet did not bring out a V8 until 1955), and offering excellent performance (10–30mph in 4·6sec) for a very reasonable price. The cheapest model in 1932, the V8's year of introduction, sold for only $460. It quickly became a favourite with hot-rodders in the United States, and with builders of trials specials in Great Britain. **Illus. 144** shows a cut-down 1932 Model 18 roadster storming a hill during a British trial, *c.* 1938; the next car awaiting its turn is an Allard, itself a Ford-based make.

145. Three Ford V8s, from left to right: 1935 Model 48 roadster; 1932 Model 18 tourer; 1934 Model 40 roadster (USA)

In **illus. 145** are three V8s, a 1935 Model 48 roadster, a 1932 Model 18 tourer, and a 1934 Model 40 roadster, in a West Hants Motor Club relay trial.

Illus. 146 shows two 1935 Model 48 convertible sedans; this style was a development of the traditional four-door touring car, but with wind-up side windows. By the mid-1930s it was quite a rare body style, and represented a small proportion of total sales. Ford still offered a phaeton (with side curtains) which cost $580, compared with $750 for the convertible sedan. Another low-production body style, but one that was growing in popularity, was the station wagon. **Illus. 147** is a 1938 Model 81A 'woodie', of which 6012 were made that year, out of a total Ford V8 production of 410,048 cars.

146. Two 1935 Ford V8 Model 48 convertible sedans (USA)

147. 1938 Ford V8 Model 8IA station wagon (USA)

148. 1933 Hupmobile 3·7-litre coupé (USA)

Hupmobile had been a successful medium-sized car producer during the 1920s and was usually in the top dozen of the production league. A takeover of the Chandler plant in 1929 had given the firm greater facilities, but the Depression hit sales badly, and in 1933 they reached a low of 7316, compared with 65,857 in 1928. The 1933 cars, of which a coupé is shown (illus. 148), had attractive, if conventional lines, but in the following year Hupmobile adopted an aerodynamic style with headlights faired into the bonnet sides, which helped to boost sales a little. However, the company could not compete with the mass producers and was out of business by 1940.

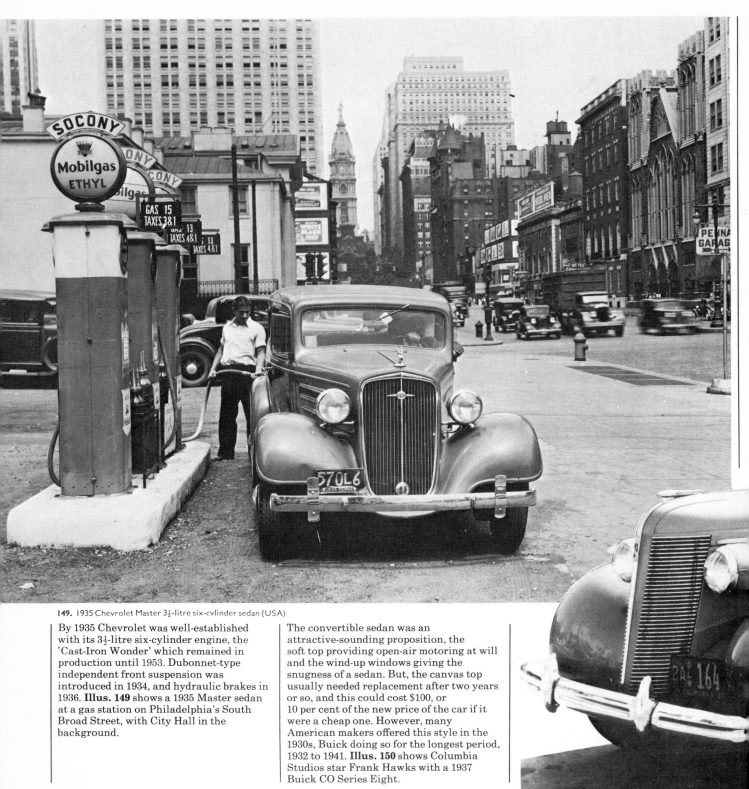

149. 1935 Chevrolet Master 3½-litre six-cylinder sedan (USA)

By 1935 Chevrolet was well-established with its 3½-litre six-cylinder engine, the 'Cast-Iron Wonder' which remained in production until 1953. Dubonnet-type independent front suspension was introduced in 1934, and hydraulic brakes in 1936. **Illus. 149** shows a 1935 Master sedan at a gas station on Philadelphia's South Broad Street, with City Hall in the background.

The convertible sedan was an attractive-sounding proposition, the soft top providing open-air motoring at will and the wind-up windows giving the snugness of a sedan. But, the canvas top usually needed replacement after two years or so, and this could cost $100, or 10 per cent of the new price of the car if it were a cheap one. However, many American makers offered this style in the 1930s, Buick doing so for the longest period, 1932 to 1941. **Illus. 150** shows Columbia Studios star Frank Hawks with a 1937 Buick CO Series Eight.

151. 1940 GAZ 11-40 76bhp six-cylinder convertible sedan (SU)

A Soviet variation on the convertible sedan theme, although this 1940 GAZ 11-40 (**illus. 151**) seems to have button-down sidescreens, which make it a late example of a tourer rather than a true convertible sedan. A development of the GAZ M-1 powered by a Soviet-built Model A Ford engine, the GAZ 11-40 used a 76bhp 3485cc six-cylinder unit.

152. 1930 Duesenberg Model J 6·9-litre convertible coupé (USA)

Despite the Depression which not only reduced the numbers of the rich, but made those who managed to hold onto their wealth less ready to flaunt it, luxury cars continued to sell in the United States in the 1930s, and none was more glamorous than the Duesenberg Model J with its 6882cc twin-overhead-camshaft straight-eight engine developing 265bhp. The cost of the Model J has been exaggerated in recent years—hardly any were as high as the $25,000 frequently quoted—but prices in the $12,000 to $19,000 range were not unusual. **Illus. 152** shows a 1930 Model J with Murphy convertible body, posed with film star Rosita Moreno.

150. 1937 Buick CO 5·2-litre Series Eight convertible sedan (USA)

153. 1935 Cadillac V12 6-litre town car (USA)

In addition to its well-known V8s, Cadillac made two top-line cars in the early 1930s, the 135bhp 6-litre V12 and the 165bhp 7·4-litre V16. The latter was one of only two production sixteen-cylinder cars in the world; the other was the Marmon, but this make sold far fewer sixteens than Cadillac and was out of business by 1933. Both the big Cadillacs had pushrod overhead-valve engines, each bank of cylinders having its own carburettor and ignition coil. The V12 was made from 1931 to 1937, production being 10,521 units; the V16 from 1930 to 1940 (4386 made). **Illus. 153** shows film star Jean Harlow with her 1935 V12 town car. In **illus. 154** is a V16 standard seven-passenger sedan, also dating from 1935.

154. 1935 Cadillac V16 7·4-litre seven-passenger sedan (USA)

155. 1932 Lincoln Model KB V12 7·2-litre roadster (USA)

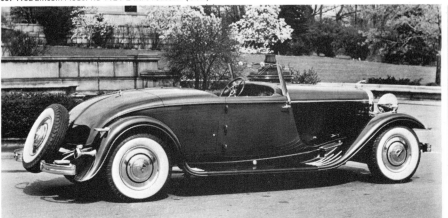

In 1932 the Lincoln company introduced its first V12, the 7·2-litre Model KB. A wide variety of bodywork was available on this 145in wheelbase chassis, the cheaper varieties being 'semi-custom' jobs built by Lincoln but based on designs from the great custom coachbuilders. The latter also built many bodies themselves, usually in very limited series approved by Edsel Ford. This unusual and extravagantly upholstered roadster by Brunn & Company of Buffalo, N.Y. (**illus. 155** and **158**), may well have been a one-off design. Brunn built many bodies for Lincoln, including personal cars for Henry Ford.

Despite the relative success of the 'senior' Packards, the company felt the need to break into a new market and in 1934 it hired an engineer from General Motors, G. T. Christopher, set up a new factory, and launched a new series of moderately priced straight eights, known as the 120. This had a 3·8-litre engine giving a maximum speed of 82mph for the sedan, and the cheapest model cost only $980, compared with $2000 for a 5·3-litre Senior Eight. The 120 boosted sales dramatically, from 6071 in 1934 to 52,256 in 1935. Two years later a still smaller Packard, the 3·6-litre six-cylinder 115, was introduced, at a base price of $860. Sales in 1937, the year of the 115 sedan shown in **illus. 156**, were 109,518, making it the best season in Packard's fifty-nine-year history.

Throughout the 1930s Packard remained one of America's most respected names, and for an expensive car it survived the Depression well, generally outselling Cadillac even in the leanest years. **Illus. 157** shows the celebrated cowboy Ken Maynard with two straight-eight Packards, a 1932 tourer and a 1931 roadster towing the horsebox. Behind is a third vehicle in his *équipe*, a Ford Model BB van.

156. 1937 Packard 115 3·6-litre sedan (USA)

157. Two straight-eight Packards: a 1932 tourer and a 1931 roadster, followed by a Ford Model BB van (USA)
158. The interior of the 1932 Lincoln

159. 1940 Packard 180 5·8-litre roadster (USA)
160. 1933 Buick with a Nordberg cabriolet body (USA/S)

By 1940 custom bodies were distinctly rare on American cars, but Packard offered a line of very handsome 'semi-custom' designs built for them by such coachbuilders as Rollson, Darrin and LeBaron. The Darrin two-door roadster was particularly attractive. The car in **illus. 159** looks very like a four-door version of the Darrin, but is in fact by Bohman & Schwartz of Pasadena, Cal.

During the 1930s there was a considerable vogue in European countries for building custom bodies on comparatively cheap American chassis. The results were often very attractive, for they combined the large, relatively slow-turning American engine with the elegance of European coachwork. As Michael Lamm, editor of *Special-Interest Autos*, said, '. . . the performance and looks of a classic but at a much more reasonable price.' Among European coachbuilders who regularly built on American chassis were Carlton, Maltby and Tickford in England; Gläser in Germany; Graber, Beutler and Langenthal in Switzerland; and Nordberg in Sweden. Curiously, Italy, the home of custom coachbuilding, did practically no work on American chassis. The photos show (**illus. 160**) a Nordberg cabriolet on a 1933 Buick chassis, and (**illus. 161**) a Dagenham Motors pillarless sedan on a 1935 Ford V8.

A step further than the custom body on a US chassis was the Anglo-American hybrid, in which the engine and chassis frame were American, but the brakes, suspension and steering were reworked, the dashboard Anglicized, and the British body given a freshly styled bonnet and grille so that the result was a new make of car. The first and most successful company to do this was Railton of Cobham, Surrey, who used the Terraplane Eight (later Hudson Eight) engine; other examples of the art included the Hudson-based Brough Superior, the Jensen and the Allard which used the Ford V8 engine, and the super-charged Lammas-Graham. Some very handsome cars were made by these small companies, but the closed models tended to become too heavy, so that their performance was inferior to that of the cheaper American product on which they were based. The photos show (**illus. 162**) a 1937 Jensen sports tourer in the Concours d'Élégance of the Welsh Rally and (**illus. 163**) a 1938 Railton Cobham saloon.

161. 1935 Ford V8 3·6-litre pillarless sedan (USA/GB)

162. 1937 Jensen 3·6-litre sports tourer (GB)

163. 1938 Railton Cobham 4·2-litre saloon (GB)

The Austin Seven continued to be Britain's most popular small car during the 1930s, and although the bulk of the cars made were saloons or cabriolets (named Ruby and Pearl respectively), many competition models were built, from road-going sports cars such as the Nippy and Speedy to the twin-ohc single-seater racing cars designed by Murray Jamieson and raced from 1936 to 1939. **Illus. 164** shows a standard 1931 Chummy tourer entered by A. C. Fairtlough in the Novices' Handicap of the B.A.R.C. Inter-Club meeting at Brooklands. Fairtlough's was the 'limit' car and finished third. **Illus. 165** is of one of the works sports Sevens known as Grasshoppers. A few of these were built in 1936 and competed successfully in most of the year's major trials but they were not sold to the public. The photo shows W. S. Sewell on Fingle Bridge Hill during the Land's End Trial.

164. 1931 Austin Seven 747cc Chummy tourer (GB)
165. 1936 Austin Seven Grasshopper 747cc sports car (GB)

The closest rival to the Austin Seven sports was the M.G. Midget which started life in 1928 as a derivation of the Morris Minor. Apart from lowered suspension, raked steering column and a light, fabric-covered two-seater sports body, it was little different from its touring progenitor, but its sporty looks and low price (£175) found it many buyers, and in its first year of production more were sold than of all previous M.G.s added together. It was the popularity of the M type Midget that led to the move from the Morris Garages' premises in Alfred Lane, Oxford, to a new factory at Abingdon, Berkshire, where M.G.s are still made today. **Illus. 166** shows a 1930 M type Midget taking part in driving tests in a 1937 Welsh Rally. The M type was succeeded by the J type in 1932, and this in turn by the P series in 1934. All these M.G.s had single-ohc engines, but in 1935 it was decided that these were too expensive, and that future Midgets would have to make do with a pushrod-overhead-valve engine shared with other cars of the Nuffield empire. Thus there appeared the TA Midget with 1292cc Wolseley Ten engine, though tuned to give 50bhp. **Illus. 167** shows a 1936 TA in the 1937 Lawrence Cup Trial.

Another line of M.G. development was represented by the Magna and Magnette series, which utilized the small six-cylinder engine of the Wolseley Hornet. **Illus. 168** shows the beginning of the line, the 1932 F type Magna, with 1271cc overhead-camshaft engine, in coupé form. Later developments were the 1087cc L type, which led to the Magnette made in sports and racing form.

166. 1930 M.G. M type Midget 847cc sports car (GB)

167. 1936 M.G. TA Midget 1292cc sports car (GB)
168. 1932 M.G. F type Magna 1271cc coupé (GB)

Closely related to the F type Magna was the Wolseley Hornet (**illus. 169**) which was literally a stretched Morris Minor. The body was identical, and so were the cylinder dimensions, only there were six of them instead of four, giving a capacity of 1271cc and necessitating a longer bonnet and therefore a wheelbase of 7ft 6½in compared with 6ft 6in of the Minor. Other improvements over the Minor included 12-volt electric system and hydraulic brakes; yet the Hornet fabric saloon illustrated cost only £175.

Another popular light sports car was the Singer Nine (**illus. 170**), made from 1933 to 1937. Singer Nines raced with some success at Le Mans, but their real forte was in trials, where two- and four-seater models did very well and frequently defeated the M.G. teams. The photo shows three 1935 works team cars awaiting their turn at Nailsworth Ladder in Gloucestershire.

169. 1930 Wolseley Hornet 1271cc fabric saloon (GB)

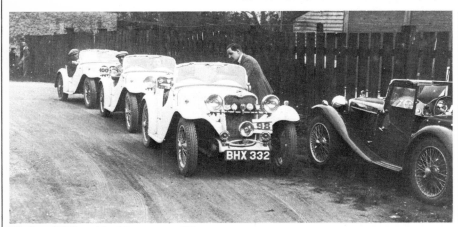

170. Three 1935 Singer Nine 972cc sports cars (GB)

A 1931 Riley Colonial Nine tourer (**illus. 171**), otherwise known as the WD (War Department) model as the original series was developed for the War Office. The cars were also sold to the public, and had oversize wheels, lower rear axle ratio, increased ground clearance and strengthened chassis frame. One was entered by Rupert St George Riley (no member of the family that made the cars) in the 1933 Monte Carlo Rally, but retired between Vienna and Budapest.

In 1938 Riley became part of the Nuffield Organization, and the last prewar models began to lose their individuality, a process that was continued until the name disappeared in 1969, by which time it was nothing more than a Mini with a Riley grille and built-out boot. The 1939-40 cars retained the high-camshaft four-cylinder engine in 1½- and 2½-litre form, but the preselector gear change was replaced by an ordinary synchromesh box, and the bodies were heavier-looking than before. **Illus. 172** shows a 1939 1½-litre saloon at a Concours d'Élégance at Brighton, Sussex, followed by a Jaguar cabriolet and a Wolseley Ten saloon.

172. 1939 Riley 1½-litre saloon (GB)

171. 1931 Riley Colonial Nine tourer (GB)

175. 1939 Jaguar 3½-litre saloon (GB)

173. 1934 S.S.1 20hp saloons and coupés (GB)

Evolution of the Jaguar: one of Britain's best-known postwar cars began life in 1931 as the S.S.I, an exceptionally low-slung long-bonneted coupé powered by a 2-litre 16hp Standard engine in a frame also made by Standard, but to the designs of William Lyons, the 'father' of the S.S. This was later supplemented by a 2½-litre 20hp engine, and larger bodies were provided in the shape of a close-coupled four-seater coupé, open tourer, and Airline saloon. **Illus. 173** shows the first batch of S.S.Is for export to the United States outside the factory in October 1934. An Airline saloon heads the column, followed by a coupé, two tourers and more coupés. These cars have right-hand drive. It was not until after World War II that Jaguar became sufficiently export-minded to make left-hand drive cars. As well as the six-cylinder S.S. cars, there was a smaller model known as the S.S.II powered by four-cylinder Standard Nine, Ten or Twelve engines. In 1936 a new overhead-valve cylinder head was designed by Harry Weslake and Bill Heynes for the 2½-litre engine; this was incorporated in a new four-door saloon christened the S.S. Jaguar, and in a two-seater sports car, the S.S. 100. Both these cars later became available with a 125bhp 3½-litre engine and were remarkably good value at £445. **Illus. 174** shows a 2½-litre S.S.100 during the 1937 Welsh Rally, in which the make won the team prize, and **illus. 175** a 1939 3½-litre saloon.

174. 1937 S.S. Jaguar 100 2½-litre sports car (GB)

176. 1938 Morris Series II Eight four-door saloon (GB)

177 1939 Morris Series E Eight two-door saloon (GB)

Austin Seven, Ford Model Y and Morris Eight took a large part of the British under-1000cc small-car market in the 1930s. The Morris was the last to appear, being launched for 1935 as a replacement for the Minor. It had a 918cc four-cylinder side-valve engine that was to last well into the era of the postwar Minor, and was available with four body styles–two- and four-door saloons, and two- and four-seater tourers. In 1937 came the Series II of which the four-door saloon is shown in **illus. 176**; pressed steel in place of wire wheels were the main external differences. In October 1938 came the Series E which had the same engine with power boosted from 23·5 to 29·5bhp and a slightly wider chassis. The body was totally new and was the most modern-looking on any British small car, with no running boards, and headlights faired into the wings. Body styles were two- and four-door saloons and a four-seater tourer; the saloons were revived after the war, but the price of a two-door had gone up from £139 in 1939 to £314 in 1946. **Illus. 177** shows a 1939 two-door Series E saloon.

One of the most original mass-produced European cars of the 1930s was the FIAT 500, nicknamed 'Topolino' (Mickey Mouse). Introduced in April 1936, it was the smallest FIAT ever made, with an engine of only 569cc capacity. However, it was no freakish cyclecar, for it had a four-cylinder watercooled power unit placed ahead of the radiator, a four-speed synchromesh gearbox and hydraulic brakes. On 13bhp it could reach 55mph, and tuned models were considerably faster. The only body style available in its native Italy was a two-seater, with or without the roll top shown in **illus. 178**, but for the British market a four-seater saloon was made. Including the overhead-valve 500B and 500C models, the Topolino was made until 1954, total production being 498,384. It was also built under licence in France as the Simca Cinq and Six, and in Germany as the N.S.U. Exports took it to almost every country in the world. The United States, at that time very far from small-car minded, took 434 Topolinos in 1938–9, which made it the best-selling imported car.

178. 1936 FIAT 500 569cc two-seater (I)

Another Italian car that earned itself an excellent reputation abroad as well as at home was the Lancia Aprilia (**illus. 179**). It was the last design of the company's founder, Vincenzo Lancia, and marked a return to integral construction which he had pioneered on the 1922 Lambda. The engine was a narrow-angle V4 of 1352cc capacity and suspension was independent all round, a feature not found on any British family cars of the time. Like the FIAT 500, the Aprilia survived the war, being made until 1949.

179. 1939 Lancia Aprilia 1352cc saloon (I)

General Motors' two European bridgeheads, the British Vauxhall and the German Opel companies, made a wide range of cars with quite a number of points in common. These included integral construction, introduced by Opel on the 1935 Olympia and by Vauxhall on the 1938 Ten, and Dubonnet-type independent front suspension, used on Opel's Super Six (**illus. 180**) and Vauxhall's Fourteen (**illus. 181**). The Opel had a short-stroke engine of 2½ litres compared with the Vauxhall's 1·8 litres, which gave it a good 10mph advantage in top speed, yet on the British market the two cars sold for the same price in standard form. This was a result of the Nazi government's subsidized-exports plan, which led to a 1074cc Opel Kadett costing only £135 in 1938. The Vauxhall illustrated had a drophead coupé body by Grosvenor, which added about £33 to the regular price. In 1939 the Fourteen engine was mated to an integral construction six-light saloon body similar in general conception to that of the Ten. The result was the Model J (seen in **illus. 182** overleaf during the 1939 RAC Brighton Rally) which was part of the postwar Vauxhall programme and was made until the introduction of the Velox series in the summer of 1948.

180. 1937 Opel Super Six 2½-litre cabriolet (D)

181. 1938 Vauxhall Fourteen 1·8-litre foursome coupé (GB)

182. 1939 Vauxhall Model J Fourteen 1·8-litre saloon (GB)

183. 1939 Škoda Superb 2·9-litre saloon (CS)

The Czechoslovakian Škoda armaments company began car production in 1922 with licence-built Hispano-Suizas and during the 1930s made some advanced small cars with backbone frames and all-independent suspension. The top model of the range was the six-cylinder Superb, originally a 2½-litre, later enlarged to 2·9 litres and then 3·1 litres. This shared the backbone frame of the smaller cars, and, like them, had an ohv engine from 1937 onwards. **Illus. 183** shows a 1939 Superb saloon which was available with 2·9-litre 65bhp or 3·1-litre 80bhp engine. It was revived very briefly after the war.

The Bentley of the 1930s was a less obviously sporting car than that of the previous decade, as the company had been taken over by Rolls-Royce in 1931 and all subsequent Bentleys shared components with the smaller Rolls models. Advertised as 'The Silent Sports Car', the 3½-litre and its successors the 4¼-litre Bentleys were admirable high-speed touring cars with a maximum speed of over 90mph. In 1939 an overdrive top gear was provided for the 4¼, which though no faster, reduced the engine's revs at top speed from 4500 to about 4200rpm. The 1940 Mark V models had

185. Left: 1939 Bugatti Type 57 3·3-litre four-door saloon; right: 1939 Bugatti Type 57C 3·3-litre coupé (F)

184. 1938 Bentley 4¼-litre drophead coupé (GB)

coil-and-wishbone independent front suspension inherited from the Rolls Phantom III, but few of these were made because of the outbreak of war. **Illus. 184** shows a 1938 4¼-litre Vanden Plas drophead coupé at Brooklands in 1939. This body was built by Vanden Plas for the 1938 Scottish Show.

Bugattis of the 1920s had ranged from out-and-out racing cars (Type 35) to the elephantine 12¾-litre Royale, but for the leaner times of the 1930s Ettore Bugatti concentrated on the *grand routier* or fast tourer. The bulk of production from 1934 onwards was devoted to the Type 57, with twin-overhead-camshaft 3·3-litre engine developing 135bhp, or 160bhp in supercharged form, when it was known as

the Type 57C. There were also low-chassis models known as Types 57S and 57SC respectively. In **illus. 185** are two cars owned by those great Bugatti fanciers, the Cholmondeley family; on the left Lady Cholmondeley's Type 57 four-door saloon and on the right Lord Cholmondeley's Type 57C coupé.

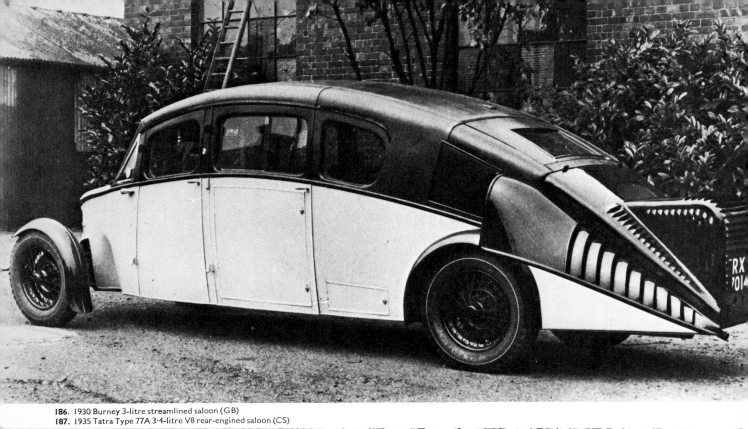

186. 1930 Burney 3-litre streamlined saloon (GB)
187. 1935 Tatra Type 77A 3·4-litre V8 rear-engined saloon (CS)

During the 1930s streamlining became an important factor in body design for the first time, though a good deal of it was of more interest to the styling and sales departments than to the engineers. A teardrop design had been built on an Alfa Romeo chassis as long ago as 1914, and the German doctor Paul Jaray had made a number of bodies on aerodynamic principles on Apollo, Ley and other chassis in the 1920s. One of the first production cars employing a streamlined body was the Burney (**illus. 186**) designed by the airship engineer Sir Dennistoun Burney. It had an exceptionally long wheelbase of 13ft 5in and behind this projected a straight-eight engine made either by Beverley or Lycoming. At a price of £1500 it is hardly surprising that only twelve Burney Streamlines were sold, one customer being the Prince of Wales. Nevertheless a speed of 80mph from 80bhp and a 2-ton car showed that aerodynamics were worth studying. A rear-engined car that went into more serious production was the Czechoslovakian Tatra; it appeared in 1934 with a 2·9-litre aircooled V8 engine, later enlarged to 3·4 litres as the Type 77A (**illus. 187**). Maximum speed was over 90mph, but weak points were handling and poor rearward vision.

The best-known attempt to combine streamlining with mass production was the Chrysler Airflow, of which over 26,000 were made from 1934 to 1937. All Chrysler's Airflows used straight-eight engines, of 4·9, 5·3 and 6·3 litres, but some six-cylinder Airflows were produced under the De Soto name. Apart from the styling, the most radical feature was the all-steel integral construction, with a cagelike steel-girder frame that carried the body panels. The Airflow was also the first American car to use Borg-Warner automatic overdrive. Unfortunately the radical styling did not attract customers and Chrysler watered down the streamlining in 1935–7 models, giving them a silly little prow in a futile attempt to render them less revolutionary in appearance. **Illus. 188** shows a 1934 Model CU sedan. An obvious attempt to cash in on the supposed popularity of the Airflow was the British Singer Airstream (**illus. 189**), launched about nine months after the Chrysler, on the ordinary Singer Eleven chassis. Despite publicity gimmicks such as the sale of a fleet of Airstreams to members of Jack Payne's dance band, fewer than 300 of the cars were sold.

Gabriel Voisin's aerodynamic cars of the 1930s were typical of this idiosyncratic designer: not particularly beautiful, but designed from first principles without regard to customers' tastes. Nevertheless, several examples were sold of the 1935 Aérodyne saloon (**illus. 190**), powered by a

188. 1934 Chrysler Model CU Airflow 4·4-litre sedan (USA)

189. 1934-5 Singer Airstream 11hp saloon (GB)

190. 1935 Voisin Aérodyne 3-litre six-cylinder saloon (F)

standard Voisin 3-litre six-cylinder
sleeve-valve engine, and there was a later,
even more streamlined, Aérosport coupé.
Illus. 191 shows a Czechoslovakian Walter
Standard S 3-litre of 1934, with special
streamlined drophead coupé body. **Illus. 192**
is yet another American offering on the
theme, the 1936 Lincoln Zephyr sedan.
Like the Chrysler Airflow, the Zephyr had
integral construction and was the first
entry by the prestigious Lincoln company
into the medium-priced field. It had a
comparatively small V12 engine of 4·4 litres
and cost only $1300 – it was the world's
cheapest V12.

191. 1934 Walter Standard S 3-litre drophead coupé (CS)

193. 1938 Graham Custom 3½-litre convertible (USA)

The 1938–9 Graham Custom series was
unusual not only in its 'sharknose' styling
with a grille that actually leaned forward
instead of sloping backwards, but also in its
use of a supercharger. After the demise of
the Auburn in 1937, Graham was the only
American company to offer this feature.
Illus. 193 shows a Graham at the 1938 Paris
Salon with a custom-built convertible body.
The company itself never built open models
in this series. Finally, in illus. **194**, we have
an opulently curved convertible on the
Czech Aero 50 2-litre two-stroke chassis.
The coachwork is by Sodomka, then
Czechoslovakia's leading bodybuilders.
The stylist seems to have been looking
hard at Saoutchik's efforts on Delahaye
chassis, particularly in the wing lines with
enclosed front and back wheels, and the
grille is very reminiscent of the
1939 Hudson.

194. 1939 Aero 50 2-litre cabriolet (CS)

192. 1936 Lincoln Zephyr V12 4·4-litre sedan (USA)

COMMERCIAL VEHICLES

INTRODUCTION

The load-carrying commercial vehicle was a comparative latecomer on the transport scene, mainly because of the efficiency and comprehensiveness of railway networks, which by the 1890s had reached their zenith in most industrialized countries. The limited amount of goods transport on the roads was catered for by the horse or the steam traction engine, working at a maximum speed of no more than 4mph. When the lorry did appear, it was an adaptation of the early passenger car, and as the latter carried at the most no more than four people, the amount of space for the accommodation of goods was strictly limited. The first step towards a specialized commercial vehicle was taken by the German Daimler company who, in 1896, moved the driver forward so that he sat at the very front of the vehicle, with the whole of the rest of the body available for load. The engine was at the back anyway, so there was no problem of accommodating it, but when Daimler moved the power unit to the front in 1898 the driver sat above it, and later behind a short bonnet. The driver-over-engine position, later known as cab-over-engine (coe) in America and forward control in Britain, became popular for a while as it did allow for a greater load space in the same wheelbase as normal control. But for reasons of comfort and safety it gave way to the carlike bonneted arrangement by about 1914 (earlier in Europe), only to be revived in the 1920s when the driver and his mate sat beside the engine rather than on top of it. In the early days commercial development paralleled that of the passenger car, with four-cylinder engines coming in after 1900 and continually growing in size, although there were also the light vans which used single or two-cylinder engines as in contemporary light cars, and even smaller than these were the trade carriers based on tricars.

The foregoing paragraph applies to internal-combustion-engined vehicles, but the steam commercial vehicle followed paths of its own, quite separate from those of steam passenger cars. Contrary to popular belief, the steam wagon was not simply a load-carrying version of the traction engine, despite a superficial resemblance between the latter and the overtype wagon. The earliest steam wagons, made by Thornycroft and Leyland, were undertypes, with the engine mounted on the chassis frame, and a vertical boiler either ahead of, or behind the driver. Like the forward-control lorry, this arrangement gave maximum load-carrying space, but the engines were not easily accessible, and the vertical boilers were not always efficient producers of steam. The alternative arrangement, which was introduced by Foden in 1901, was the horizontal or locomotive boiler, with the engine mounted above it. This layout was used by some fifteen British makers and continued in production until the late 1920s. Just to confuse matters, there were a few designs with horizontal boilers and undertype engines, made from 1905 to 1909, but they were never numerous or particularly successful. Like the traction engine, the early steam wagons had steel tyres, these giving way to solid rubber in the years up to 1914, and to pneumatics in the late 1920s. Load capacity of a typical overtype was 5-6 tons, and its working life could be anything up to twenty or more years, much longer than the average petrol-engined lorry.

The steam wagon was far more widely used in Britain than in any other country, thanks to an abundant supply of cheap coal, and was only driven from the roads by the arrival of the diesel engine in 1928, and legislation on maximum weight per axle in 1933, which made them prohibitively expensive to run. The last steam wagons for the British market were built by Sentinel in 1939, although this company fulfilled an export order for Argentina as late as 1950.

If Britain was the home of the steam wagon, the electric vehicle had its widest following in America, where enormous slow-moving forward-control trucks with capacities of up to 10 tons were used for a variety of work from 1898 until the early 1920s. The traditional drawback of limited range was not a disadvantage for city work, and the electric trucks seldom ventured into the countryside. Large electrics, often of American origin, were popular in Britain during the 1920s, and the G.V. company of Birmingham even made an articulated six-wheeler with a 10-ton capacity. In the early 1930s the electric took on a new role, replacing the horse for house-to-house deliveries of milk and bread. These vans, or open-sided milk floats, were much smaller than their predecessors, with capacities of about a quarter to half a ton, and were direct ancestors of similar vehicles so widely used today. They were made in smaller numbers in America up to 1942, but the greater distances in that country made the internal-combustion engine more desirable, and led to a peculiarly American vehicle, the multi-stop delivery, often with a standing position for the driver. Electrics were also widely used on the Continent, particularly in Germany, for municipal and postal work, but have largely been superseded since World War II.

By 1914 the motor truck was in use in almost every country of the world for a wide variety of purposes, although still generally restricted to journeys of less than 50 miles. As with the motor bus, it was a feeder to the railways rather than a rival, but this was to change in the 1920s when long-distance trucking first became a serious proposition on both sides of the Atlantic. Improved roads were one reason for this, but there were also important developments in design which increased carrying capacity. Up to World War I no lorry had more than two axles, and as the wheelbase of such a vehicle could not be extended indefinitely the only solution was to add another axle, or to make an articulated vehicle with tractor and single-axle trailer. The latter arrangement had been pioneered by the Thornycroft company with its steam six-wheeler of 1898, but this had no immediate successors, and it was not until Charles Martin of York, Pennsylvania, designed the Knox-Martin three-wheeled tractor/trailer unit that the articulated vehicle came onto the market. Knox followed this with a four-wheeled tractor in 1918, and in 1920 Scammell of London became the first British manufacturer to offer a six-wheel articulated lorry. This could carry an 8-ton load with an engine that was no larger than those used for 5-ton rigid four-wheelers. The artic was taken up by several other manufacturers such as the trailer makers, Carrimore, who combined with Leyland to make the Carrimore-Lynx. The rigid six-wheeler, with a pair of axles at the rear, was pioneered by the Goodyear Tire & Rubber Company of Akron, Ohio, largely to publicize their new pneumatic tyres, and was taken up during the 1920s by many makers of trucks and buses in both America and Europe, including steam-wagon firms such as Sentinel, Foden and Garrett. The average carrying capacity of a rigid

six-wheeler was 12 tons, and to improve on this the rigid eight was developed, with a pair of steering axles at the front, as well as the driven axles at the rear. This layout was first used by the steam-wagon makers, Sentinel, in 1929, and was later taken up by most British heavy-vehicle firms, such as A.E.C., Albion, Foden, Leyland and Thornycroft. It was hardly seen in America or on the Continent, although within the last few years a growing number of European firms have turned to the rigid four-axle layout.

The other major development of the inter-war years was the adoption of the compression-ignition, or diesel, engine. This had been tested on a lorry in 1909, and was put into production by the German M.A.N. company in 1924. The diesel had the advantage of using cheap fuel, but early engines were difficult to start; and the British Kerr-Stuart of 1929 needed a 4hp petrol engine to start it. By the early 1930s a growing number of heavy-vehicle makers were turning to the diesel engine, either developing their own, as did Crossley, A.E.C. and Leyland, or buying from Gardner who supplied oil engines to a variety of firms. In America White brought out an opposed-piston horizontal six oil engine in 1932, following it with a horizontal twelve. However, an abundance of cheap petrol in America meant that most heavy trucks continued to use petrol engines until comparatively recent times.

The bus has a much longer history than the goods vehicle, dating back to the steamers of Goldsworthy Gurney and Walter Hancock, which were running in London in the 1830s. However, there was no continuity for the early steamers had disappeared before 1840, and it was to be over fifty years before road-going passenger vehicles were made again. As with goods vehicles, electricity and steam power were experimented with, a battery-powered double-decker bus being tried in London in 1889. In Paris and other French cities de Dion-Bouton steam buses were used in small numbers from 1894 onwards, and other French steam buses included Weidknecht and Scotte, the latter being used in conjunction with a trailer. Because of the widespread use of tramways and of horse buses, it was some time before the motor bus became established in major cities. In London, for example, there were sporadic services operated from 1899 onwards, but as late as 1905 the total number of buses running was only twenty. New York had even fewer, having made unsuccessful experiments with battery-powered buses on which the operators never made a cent of profit. By 1914, however, the picture had changed completely, and the horse bus had almost disappeared; this was due to improvements in design, and particularly standardization which led to easier maintenance and therefore lower fares, and also to the enterprise of operating companies. Most urban horse buses had been double-deckers, and consequently motor buses followed suit, although not necessarily for long. London, of course, has used double-deckers up to the present day, and so has Berlin, and New York ran them until 1953.

But in Paris the double-decker was considered dangerous, and abandoned before 1914, only to be revived in the mid-1960s. Despite the pioneering efforts of the local authority at Widnes, Lancashire, with a closed top in 1909, open tops remained the rule until the 1920s, and even when the upper deck was enclosed, open staircases lasted for several years longer.

In rural areas the motor bus played a more important role than in towns, for here horse buses were much rarer, and villages that did not have a railway station were almost completely cut off from the towns. The best that the poorer inhabitants could hope for in the way of transport was a seat on the carrier's cart, along with furniture and any other goods he might be carrying. The country bus not only took passengers to the towns, but also carried milk to the station, and collected the mails. One of its most important roles was to act as a feeder to the railways, and many country bus routes were operated by the railway companies who, in at least one case, the Great Northern Railway, built their own buses. Like goods vehicles, buses did not on the whole operate over long distances; charabancs tended to radiate from seaside and mountain resorts rather than run from industrial cities to the resorts as they have done in more recent years.

Up to the early 1920s bus design followed that of the lorry, and most buses were built on goods-vehicle chassis. Gradually the purpose-built bus chassis appeared, the chief feature of which was the lowered frame which enabled the vehicle to be entered via only one step. This not only made life easier for the passenger but lowered the centre of gravity and improved greatly the vehicle's appearance. Some of the single-decker buses and coaches of 1925–30

achieved a standard of appearance which has never been improved on since. As with lorries, forward control and three axles came in during the 1920s, many of the forward-control buses having a half cab on the offside of the engine. Seating capacity of a three-axle single-decker such as the Karrier WL6 was up to thirty-five; double-deckers such as the A.E.C. LS of 1927 seated up to seventy-two. One example of the LS, used to carry workmen from A.E.C.'s Walthamstow factory to the new premises at Southall, carried 102 passengers on occasions. In America the most important step in bus design was taken in 1927 by the newly formed Twin Coach Company of Kent, Ohio, which built a remarkable machine with two four-cylinder Waukesha engines mounted under the floor behind each front wheel. Radiators were at the side, and so front and rear ends of the bus could be symmetrical, with doors ahead of the front and behind the rear axles. The Twin Coach was gradually developed over the years, but even the prototype has a strikingly modern appearance. Later underfloor-engined buses were made in England by A.E.C. (the Q type), and in Germany by Büssing and Mercedes-Benz. In America Yellow Coach built a range of rear-engined coaches for Greyhound Lines from 1936 onwards which again look little dated even today.

The long-distance coach became commonplace by 1930, offering, as it still does today, excellent value compared with the railways, at the cost of a longer time for the journey. A short-lived fashion of the late 1920s was the sleeper coach, of which one of the best-known was the Land Liners Ltd service operated with Guy three-axle double-deckers between London and Manchester. These had seats convertible to bunks for thirty-one passengers, cooking facilities and a toilet. In America, Pickwick Stages Lines built their own sleeper coaches, but in neither country was the system popular. They were less comfortable than trains, and passengers who wanted to make really long journeys by coach preferred to spend the night in a hotel. Excursions by coach also blossomed in the 1920s, not only charabanc trips on public holidays but tours of several days' duration. Continental coach trips from Britain began in 1920, and in 1925 were extended as far afield as Germany and Spain. In 1935 you could have a twenty-one-day coach tour of Russia.

195. 1892 Le Blant steam van (F)

TWO-AXLED LOAD CARRIERS

The earliest motor competitions were open to both private and commercial vehicles, as they were demonstrations of the new motive power rather than races or rallies as they were to become later. These photos show two goods vehicles in such events. **Illus. 195** is an 1892 Le Blant steam van owned by the Paris store *La Belle Jardinière*, entered in the 1894 Paris-Rouen Trial; **illus. 196** is of an 1896 Arnold van in the Emancipation Run from London to Brighton, held in November 1896. The Le Blant required two people to drive it, a steersman at the front and a mechanic, who looked after the lubricator and stoking, at the rear. They communicated by speaking tube, but it was said that 'there was a lack of unity in their movements, which did not tend to the efficient running of the car'.

197. 1898 Cannstatt-Daimler lorry (D)

One of the first vehicles designed specifically for load carrying was the Cannstatt-Daimler lorry of 1896. It used the same rear-mounted V-twin engine as the contemporary cars, but the driver was seated at the very front of the vehicle to give maximum load space. **Illus. 197** is of an 1898 lorry from the same makers. The engine is now in front, but the forward control position is continued, with the driver sitting over the engine.

196. 1896 Arnold petrol van (GB)

198. 1899 British Daimler four-cylinder Post Office van (GB)

Among the more unusual loads carried by early trucks is this crated aircraft (**illus. 199**), which has evidently been brought over from France to England to take part in a flying competition, *c.* 1911. Note *haut* and *bas* clearly marked on the side of the crate to ensure that the valuable contents did not become upended. The English contractor, G. A. Duff of Wimbledon, styles himself 'aeroplane remover', but this specialized business would hardly have kept him and his five men in work unless he had gone in for more mundane removals as well.

Another forward-control vehicle, this time a British Daimler van with four-cylinder engine (**illus. 198**), supplied to the Post Office in 1899. Note the gilled-tube radiator mounted behind the rear axle. This did not function at all well, with the result that the vans were returned to the factory after a few months' service. In modified form, the radiators were mounted on the roof. A similar chassis was used for the first shooting brake supplied to the Prince of Wales.

199. c. 1911 truck carrying aircraft (GB)

200. c. 1913 Autocarrier three-wheeler and Thornycroft 3-ton lorry (GB)

201. 1911 Burrell 5-ton steam wagon (GB)

202. 1907 Yorkshire Patent Steam Wagon Company steam vans (GB)

Two contrasting vehicles operated by the Great Western Railway, photographed in about 1913 (**illus. 200**). In the foreground is an Autocarrier three-wheeled parcel van, of which the GWR operated three, two for parcel delivery and one for conveying advertising literature. Made by the company that today makes A.C. sports cars, the Autocarrier was very popular for retail delivery work of all kinds, and was produced from 1904 to 1914. Behind it is a 3-ton Thornycroft lorry; this make was particularly favoured by the Great Western, many different models being used up to, and after 1949, when the company was nationalized and became British Railways (Western Region).

The steam wagon was a peculiarly British machine, being made in considerable numbers by some sixty-five firms from the turn of the century to the early 1930s. Few steamers of any importance were made in other European countries, or in the United States. The photographs show three main types of wagon: the overtype or locomotive boiler, the transverse boiler, and the vertical-boiler undertype. **Illus. 201** is a 1911 Burrell 5-ton overtype, made by a famous firm from Thetford, Norfolk, that built overtypes from 1911 to 1932. The overtype, whose best-known exponent was Foden, had the advantage of greater accessibility to the engine, but the long boiler inevitably meant that there was less load-carrying space than with the undertype. The transverse boiler was a speciality of the Yorkshire Patent Steam Wagon Company, who made wagons exclusively of this design from 1903 to 1937. The engine was in the undertype position, each cylinder being placed outside its adjacent frame member, and final drive was by a train of gears up to 1908, and by chain thereafter, except for a few late models that had shaft drive. **Illus. 202** shows four Yorkshire vans lined up on the Embankment in London for the annual parade of commercial vehicles on 14 December 1907. The undertype had a vertical boiler mounted either ahead of, or behind, the driver, and the engine mounted on the frame; **Illus. 203** (overleaf) is of a Leyland undertype of about 1908 at a Lancashire colliery.

204. 1900 Riker 5-ton electric truck (USA)

205. *c.* 1908-11 Leyland 2½-ton lorry (GB)

Just as the steamer was typically British, so the heavy electric truck was a peculiarly American vehicle. Its heyday was from the early 1900s to about 1925. Carrying anything up to 10 tons, enormous solid-tyred trucks crept slowly and silently around American cities on a wide variety of work from beer delivery to coal hauling. The Curtis Publishing Company of Philadelphia continued to use heavy electrics until well into the 1950s. **Illus. 204** is a 1900 5-ton Riker electric.

203. *c.* 1908 Leyland undertype boiler steam wagon (GB)

In 1904 the Leyland company built its first petrol-engined lorry, and slowly this side of the business began to overtake the steamers in importance, though the two types were made side by side until 1926. Petrol lorries were made in two varieties, forward control (**illus. 205**) and normal control (**illus. 206**). The former was chiefly available in sizes up to 3 tons; the bonneted models carried between 3 and 5 tons. Loads of over 5 tons were left to steam until well after World War I. Like many commercial-vehicle makers, Leyland was prepared to be flexible with customers' orders, and would make larger forward-control, or smaller normal-control vehicles if asked to. The normal-control lorry was developed into the wartime Subsidy A type lorry.

A specialized type of American truck was the low-loading dray whose exceptionally low floor enabled heavy loads to be accommodated with less difficulty than on the conventional higher-floored truck. Two makes in particular concentrated on this kind of truck, Doane and MacDonald, both of San Francisco. Some were very long-lived; this Waukesha-engined Doane of *c.* 1916 (**illus. 207**) was still in use in Portland, Ore., in 1953, when it was reported that there were at least ten others of similar vintage operating on the West Coast. Maximum capacity was 20 tons, an exceptional figure for a two-axle truck.

206. *c.* 1912 Leyland 4-ton lorry (GB)
207. *c.* 1916 Doane 6-ton low-loading truck (USA)

208. 1910 Ford Model T postal van (USA)

The Ford Model T was used for a variety of commercial work soon after its introduction, although a specifically goods-carrying chassis was not introduced by Ford until 1917, with the Model TT. **Illus. 208** is not, as might be supposed, a dogcatcher's delight from a Marx Brothers' film, but a postal van with locally built bodywork, used in Madras, India, in about 1910. **Illus. 209** shows a more conventionally bodied truck in use in Britain in 1914. Its load-carrying capacity, in British terms, was 7½cwt (840lb).

114

209. 1914 Ford Model T 7½cwt truck (USA)

210. 1915 Lanchester 38hp chassis with RNAS truck body (GB)

The Lanchester company is not normally thought of in connection with commercial vehicles, but it supplied a number of 38hp chassis fitted with truck bodies to the Royal Naval Air Service in 1915 (**illus. 210**).

These were service vehicles to the squadrons of Lanchester armoured cars also used by the RNAS. They were employed on the Russian front, where the high speed of both armoured cars and service vehicles

enabled them to be rushed from one weak spot to another of a front that ran from Petrograd to the Caucasus.

211. 1918 Liberty 5-ton truck (USA)

One of the most significant designs to emerge from World War I was the American standardized 5-ton truck, known as the Class B or Liberty. This was developed by the Gramm-Bernstein

Company of Lima, Ohio, in 1917, and manufactured by this concern and fourteen other companies. The trucks carried the letters 'USA' on the radiators, but were more commonly known as the

Liberty. Many went into civilian use after the war, such as this one (**illus. 211**) photographed in London in 1924, and the design was the origin of the French Willème lorry.

115

212. *c.* 1920 Foden overtype steam wagon (GB)

Two British steam wagons of the 1920s, a
Foden overtype (**illus. 212**) and a Garrett
undertype 6-tonner (**illus. 213**). The Foden
was by far the best known of all the
overtype designs, and several thousand
were made between 1900 and 1931. This one
has a platform body with a container on it.
Note the ample supplies of coal carried on
the cab roof. The Garrett undertype
appeared in 1922 and was made in small
numbers until 1931, being enlarged to an
8-tonner in 1924 and supplemented by a
rigid six-wheeler in 1926. Both four- and
six-wheelers were direct rivals to the
equivalent Sentinel models, but although
close in price they were not so reliable.

213. *c.* 1922-3 Garrett 6-ton undertype steam wagon (GB)

214. 1920 N.A.G. electric lorries (D)

215. c. 1924 G.V. 6-ton electric lorries (GB)

The electric commercial vehicle continued
to flourish in the 1920s, while the electric
private car became practically extinct.
A few had dummy bonnets, such as the pair
of German N.A.G. lorries in service in
Sweden in 1920 with a company apparently
named after Odin's fabulous steed (**illus.
214**), but the majority had forward control,
with both batteries and engines mounted
under the floor. Some quite large electrics
were made in Britain, in particular by
Garrett, Ransomes and G.V. The last-named
even made a 10-ton articulated
six-wheeler, a unique layout for an electric
vehicle. **Illus. 215** shows a fleet of 6-ton
G.V.s operated by Whitbread, the London
brewery, in the 1920s; **illus. 216** represents
the new generation of smaller electrics
that emerged in the early 1930s and still
flourishes today. It is a 15/20cwt G.V. of
1934.

216. 1934 G.V. 15/20cwt electric van (GB)

217. 1925 FIAT 509 *torpedo commerciale* (I)

A popular Continental alternative to the light van was the *commerciale*, which was a touring car convertible to a light truck. It might, or might not, have detachable seats enabling it to be used for pleasure purposes as well as business. **Illus. 217** shows a 1925 FIAT 509 *torpedo commerciale*, but the type was also made in France by Citroën, Renault and others.

218. *c.* 1919-21 A.E.C. rear-tipping lorry (GB)

219. *c.* 1922 Magirus side-tipping vehicle (D)

The first tipping vehicle was made in 1896, a Thornycroft steamer, but the type was not widely seen until after World War I. **Illus. 218** shows a British A.E.C. with the classic rear-tip body, and **illus. 219** is a German Magirus with the rarer side-tip layout. **Illus. 220** is another unusual design, an articulated tipper with a G.M.C. tractor. Note the pneumatic tyres on the front wheels, and solids on the other two axles. All these tippers were manually operated; on the Magirus the winding handles can clearly be seen. Power-operated tipping gear did not come in until some years later.

220. *c.* 1918 articulated tipper with G.M.C. tractor (USA)

221. 1915 Kelly-Springfield chain-drive truck (USA)

Once the motor vehicle was established, it became essential to transport fuel rapidly and in sufficient quantities to garages and stations all over the country. Horse-drawn tankers were used at first, but their maximum capacity was about 400 gallons, and even the earliest motor tankers could carry double that amount. Petrol was originally sold by ironmongers and general stores, but soon the big companies such as Shell and Standard Oil set up service stations specifically designed for the sale of their products. Some of the first Shell stations were in California; **illus. 221** shows a 1915 Kelly-Springfield truck at one such station. The chain-drive Kelly was a popular truck of its day, somewhat similar to the Mack Bulldog with its coal-scuttle bonnet ahead of the radiator. The Anglo-American Oil Company was set up to market Standard Oil products in Britain, and later other European countries, under the name Pratt's Motor Spirit. In **illus. 222** is a British Daimler tanker of 1924 in Anglo-American livery. Note the prominently displayed sign, 'By Appointment to His Majesty the King'.

222. 1924 British Daimler tanker (GB)

120

In **illus. 223** we have a Swiss-built Saurer combination petrol and oil tanker; petrol was carried in the main tank, and oil in the drums slung ahead of the rear wheels.

Illus. 224 shows a 1932 A.E.C. Mercury operated by the National Benzole Company refuelling a Handley-Page W.10. This is a normal road-going tanker, as specialized aircraft refuelling vehicles did not appear until just before World War II.

223. c. 1928 Saurer combination tanker (CH)
224. 1932 A.E.C. Mercury tanker (GB)

Moving complete houses was a complex task, but not beyond the capabilities of trucks of the 1920s. The photo (**illus. 225**), showing a California apartment block being moved in sections, was actually taken in 1947, when the White truck involved was well over twenty years old.

In the days before refrigerators came into widespread use, the delivery of ice, either shaved or in blocks, to commercial premises and private homes was an important task for the truck. **Illus. 226** shows a group of Fageol 2-tonners. On the Fageols, note the curved bumpers which look like extensions of the chassis frame although they are in fact separate; this was a feature of a number of American trucks of that period, including the Traffic. A characteristic peculiar to Fageols is the row of spines on the bonnet top.

225. 1920s White 6-ton truck (USA)

226. 1920-3 Fageol 2-ton trucks (USA)

Bizarre bodies designed for publicity purposes became popular just before World War I, and continued to be made throughout the inter-war era. They appeared in the form of shoes, pipes, houses and beer bottles; to mention only a few, and were often more suitable for attracting attention than for carrying goods. **Illus. 227** shows a 1925 FIAT 505F with radio-valve body. Other publicity vehicles had bodies that totally disguised the make of truck, but were not necessarily designed to represent any particular product. Examples of these are shown in **illus. 228** and **229**. The former is a 1933 Bedford and the latter a 1936 Canadian Ford articulated van. Despite the full-fronted cab, this was built on a normal control chassis and the steering wheel can be seen just ahead of the door.

227. 1925 FIAT 505F publicity van (I)

228. 1933 Bedford 30cwt van (GB)

229. 1936 Canadian Ford articulated van (CDN)

123

230. 1921 Rolls-Royce Silver Ghost publicity van (USA)

A common fate of large cars in old age was to be transformed into some form of commercial vehicle, van, bus, or occasionally fire engine. In **illus. 230** a 1921 Springfield-built Rolls-Royce Silver Ghost has by 1930 gained a pair of wheels and begun a new life as a publicity vehicle for a radio show. The 1925 35CV straight-eight Panhard in **illus. 231** spent the 1930s as a laundry van in London's East End. It made an impressive delivery van, but the fuel consumption must have been horrific compared with that of a Morris or Ford light van of equivalent carrying capacity. This Panhard later came into the hands of the collector A. W. F. Smith, and is to be rebodied as a sports tourer.

'I am a lineman for the County'; the Model A Ford was made in van and pick-up form in the same way as the Model T. This example (**illus. 232**) in telephone service in California is the roadster pick-up model which differed from the regular model in having an open cab. Larger trucks of 1½ tons and upwards capacity of this era were known as Model AA (see **illus. 263**).

231. 1925 Panhard 35CV straight-eight delivery van (F)

232. 1929 Ford Model A roadster pick-up (USA)

The American Austin was the smallest car in series production in the USA during the 1930s, and was generally similar to its British counterpart, but its disc wheels and bonnet louvres gave it an American appearance. This van version (illus. 233) was used by the Canadian branch of Joseph Lyons & Company, the well-known British tea and ice-cream makers.

233. 1930 American Austin 7cwt van (USA)

An important American development of the late 1920s was the multi-stop delivery van for house-to-house deliveries, chiefly of bread and milk. This work had been the last stronghold of the horse (in Britain, United Dairies did not retire their horses finally until 1958), and a number of designs were produced to cater for this market, which demanded above all ease of entrance and exit for the driver. Among the best-known were Divco and Pak-Age-Kar, the latter made originally by Stutz and then by Diamond T. **Illus. 234** shows a 1939 Diamond T-built model. Over a thousand multi-stop vans were made by the Twin Coach Company, better known for its buses, between 1929 and 1936, with both front- and rear-wheel drive. **Illus. 235**

234. 1939 Pak-Age-Kar Model 91 multi-stop delivery van (USA)

235. c. 1930 Twin Coach Company multi-stop delivery van (USA)

is of the larger of two models available in 1930. Twin Coach also made battery electrics, as did the Ward Motor Vehicle Company of Mount Vernon, N.Y., whose 1930 Model BD is shown in **illus. 236**. A number of special-body adaptations on ordinary chassis were also made, such as the 1937 Canadian Ford Stan-Drive van in **illus. 237**. The high roofline allowed the driver to stand at his work, which was easier than sitting when really frequent stops were involved.

An alternative to the multi-stop delivery was the mobile shop which could take a wide range of goods to the customer. **Illus. 238** shows a 1932 Bedford 30cwt butcher's shop in an industrial town in the north of England.

236. 1930 Ward Model BD electric delivery van (USA)

126

237. 1937 Canadian Ford Stan-drive van (CDN)

238. 1932 Bedford 30cwt mobile shop (GB)

127

239. 1932 Škoda Model 506 7273cc pantechnicon van (CS)

The traditional lorry of the 1920s in both Europe and America had its engine mounted under a bonnet and behind the front axle, just as in a passenger car. However, the demand for greater load space in as short a wheelbase as possible led to two important changes: a return to the cab-over-engine layout which had been almost universal in the early days, or the mounting of the engine over, or even in front of, the axle. The latter was favoured by many Continental manufacturers such as Škoda of Czechoslovakia, whose Model 506 of 1932 is shown here with an impressive pantechnicon van body (**illus. 239**). The Model 506 had a 7273cc six-cylinder engine.

240. 1936 Bedford 3-ton lorry fitted with a Brush-Koela producer-gas system (GB)

During the 1930s most European countries experimented with producer gas as an alternative fuel to petrol or diesel oil. The aims were economy and independence from imported oil, and the fuels used were either coal or charcoal. In the typical producer, carbon monoxide was generated by the passage of air through the burning fuel, and also by the admission of a small quantity of water or steam. The air was drawn through the fuel by suction from the running engine and one of the drawbacks of the system was that if the engine was running too slowly, the temperature of the fire fell below the level necessary for good gas making. Nevertheless, producer-gas lorries were made commercially in a number of countries, especially France and Germany. Despite her large reserves of coal, and the efforts of the Coal Utilization Council (which also made valiant attempts to prolong the use of steam wagons), Britain never manufactured producer-gas vehicles in series, although there were a number of experiments. **Illus. 240** shows a 1936 Bedford 3-tonner fitted with the Brush-Koela system. In France the chief exponents were the Berliet company, which even made a producer-gas passenger car, and Renault, whose *gazogène à bois* (charcoal) 6-tonner of 1939 is shown in **illus. 241. Illus. 242** and **243** show Swedish and Russian variations on the theme, the former a 1940 Scania-Vabis and the latter a GAZ-42, made from 1939 to 1941. This is clearly based on the Model A Ford, which as the GAZ-A survived in the Soviet Union long after it had gone out of production in America.

242. 1940 Scania-Vabis producer-gas lorry (S)

243. 1939-41 GAZ-42 producer-gas lorry (SU)

241. 1939 Renault 6-ton *gazogène à bois* lorry (F)

244. *c.* 1924 Ford Model T six-wheel truck (USA/GB)

RIGID-SIX AND RIGID-EIGHT LOAD CARRIERS

Up to the end of World War I, practically all commercial vehicles carried their loads on two axles, in the same way as passenger cars. However, the length of a two-axle chassis could not be extended infinitely, and the obvious solution was to add an axle at the rear. This layout was pioneered by the Goodyear Rubber Company in 1920 in order to demonstrate its large pneumatic tyres. Although this company did not make six-wheel trucks for sale, the idea was taken up a few years later by White, Safeway, and other American truck and bus makers. As well as the manufacturers of heavy trucks, there were other firms who offered six-wheel conversions of popular makes such as Ford and Chevrolet. Among these were the British Baico company whose work on the Model T Ford and Chevrolet is shown in **illus. 244** and **245** respectively.

246. 1930 Sentinel Model DG6 steam wagon (GB)

Among the first companies in Britain to turn to the rigid six were the steam-wagon builders, particularly Foden, Garrett and Sentinel. The Foden company had in fact drawn up plans for a rigid six as early as 1903, although it did not build one for sale until 1927. This had only one driven axle, the rear one being simply a load supporter. Sentinel announced its DG6 15-tonner in 1927, the rear axles were coupled by chains giving four-wheel drive, or what is now known as the 6 x 4 layout. Most DG6s ran on solid tyres, like the 1930 model in **illus. 246**, but pneumatics were

245. *c.* 1926 Chevrolet six-wheel pantechnicon (USA/GB)

also available. Later, in 1929, Sentinel pioneered the rigid eight-wheeler.

By the early 1930s the rigid six, usually with two driven axles, was part of many American manufacturers' ranges, better-known examples being Autocar, Corbitt, G.M.C., International, Mack and White. **Illus. 247** shows a 1931 White 10-tonner carrying a 4-ton elephant, Jewel, loaned by the Al G. Barnes circus to Paramount Pictures for a W. C. Fields comedy.

247. 1931 White 10-ton rigid-six truck (USA)

The 1930s successors to the Baico-Ford T six-wheelers were the Surrey and Sussex models which were not made by Ford of Dagenham, although recommended by them and advertised in their sales literature. They were manufactured by County Commercial Cars Ltd of Fleet, Hampshire, who today make special four-wheel-drive Ford-based tractors. The Surrey had a trailing rear axle; the Sussex was a 6 x 4. **Illus. 248** is of a 1933 Fordson six-wheeler derived from the Model BB. From the photograph it is not possible to say whether it is a Surrey or a Sussex.

248. 1933 Fordson 6-ton six-wheeler lorry (GB)

249. 1935 Armstrong-Saurer 14/15-ton rigid-eight lorry (GB)

250. 1935 Leyland Octopus 14/15-ton rigid-eight lorry (GB)

The logical extension to the rigid six was the rigid eight, with an additional axle at the front of the vehicle as well as the rear. Like the six-wheeler, this layout was thought of long before it was built, being the subject of a French patent as long ago as 1910, but the first company to put one into production was Sentinel in 1929. Sentinel was followed by A.E.C. in 1934, and by the outbreak of war most heavy-vehicle makers in Britain had a rigid eight in their range. The type was not popular in other countries, although the Belgian Miesse company offered one briefly, and in America a number have been made for specialized work such as carrying cement mixers. The photos show two British examples of 1935, an Armstrong-Saurer (**illus. 249**) and a Leyland Octopus (**illus. 250**), both with capacities of 14/15 tons. The Armstrong-Saurer was originally a British version of the well-known Swiss lorry, but gradually became more individual in design; no forward-control models or rigid eights were made in Switzerland.

252. 1903 Tasker 'Little Giant' 4/5-ton 30bhp light steam tractor (GB)

TRACTION ENGINES, ROAD TRACTORS AND ARTICULATED VEHICLES

The steam traction engine originated in the 1840s as a self-propelled version of the agricultural engines that had to be towed by horses from one farm to another. Early traction engines such as the Bray were used for road haulage by 1860, and from the 1880s onwards they became the standard vehicle for heavy work of all kinds, not being replaced until the appearance of really powerful diesel-engined tractors in the 1930s. Road locomotives varied in size from 30 to 100bhp, and could haul loads from 5 to 50 tons. The light general-purpose road tractor was restricted in Britain to a maximum unladen weight of 3 tons by the Locomotives on Highways Act of 1896, though this was raised to 5 tons in 1903. The incentive for keeping below this level was that the light tractor was permitted to travel at 5mph, compared with 4mph in the country and 2mph in towns for heavier vehicles. Also it could be driven by one man instead of the two insisted on by the law for the larger engines. **Illus. 251** shows a Wallis & Steevens tractor with a train of three furniture vans, taken in about 1912, and **illus. 252** is of one of the most popular light tractors, the Tasker 'Little Giant' which could easily cope with loads of 4 to 5 tons, although its engine developed no more than 30bhp.

251. *c.* 1912 Wallis & Steevens steam tractor with three furniture vans (GB)

Illus. 253 shows an Aveling & Porter traction engine owned by the local authority at Luton, Bedfordshire, towing away a single-decker tram to the scrapyard.

The most ornate form of traction engine was the showman's engine, characterized by twisted brass on the cab support columns, copper or brass hubcaps and an abundance of decorative paintwork throughout. This type also carried a dynamo ahead of the boiler to generate electricity for lighting fairground booths. The first showman's engine was made by Fowler in 1885, and the last by Foster in 1934, these two firms together with Burrell being the leading makers of the type. **Illus. 254** shows the Fowler 'King George v' (nearly all showman's engines had individual names), owned by William Haggar of Aberdare who ran a biograph, or cinema show.

253. c. 1914 Aveling & Porter steam tractor (GB)

254. 1910 Fowler 'King George V' showman's traction engine (GB)

255. 1914 Dennis four-cylinder road tractor (GB)

The petrol or diesel-engined road tractor pulling a full trailer has never been very widespread, because the articulated semi-trailer vehicle came in at about the time when the traction engine was being phased out. Nevertheless diesel road tractors are still used for the heaviest loads, when specially constructed trailers are necessary. These photos show three road tractors of different eras. **Illus. 255** is an unusual Dennis with engine mounted behind the driver, dating from 1914. Although for test purposes it is towing a British brewery trailer, it never saw service in Britain, but was sent to work for South African Railways. The enormous Laurin & Klement in **illus. 256** has a very antique appearance for its date of 1924. Built by the Czech firm who had just been taken over by Škoda, it is an artillery tractor. **Illus. 257** shows a 1929 Latil tractor with four-wheel drive and steering. Originating in France, Latils were very popular in England for road and forestry work, and were made in Letchworth from 1932 to 1939. Tractors with drawbar trailers were restricted to a maximum speed of 8mph at this time.

256. 1924 Laurin & Klement artillery tractor (CS)
257. 1929 Latil four-wheel-drive tractor (F)

The first articulated trucks to be put into production were designed by C. H. Martin and manufactured by the Knox Automobile Company of Springfield, Mass. The three-wheeled tractor in **illus. 258** was made from 1912 to 1915, and was intended primarily for drawing trailers built for horse traction. It was followed by a four-wheeler whose 'fifth-wheel' turntable design was later taken up by Scammell in Britain.

The British pioneer of the articulated three-axle layout was Scammell, of London E1 and later of Watford, Hertfordshire. The company only went ahead with the design after establishing that it would be within legal requirements, the main one being that the loading on each axle should not exceed 6 tons. If it did, the maximum speed limit would be 5mph instead of 12mph, and this would clearly have been useless for a practical lorry in 1919. As it was, the prototype Scammell could carry an 8-ton load at a speed of 18mph on the level, a considerable gain on the 5 tons carried by the average two-axle lorry of the time. An important feature of the Scammell design was that the turntable on which the trailer was mounted was carried on semi-elliptic springs attached to the tractor's rear axle, thus the wheels took the trailer's weight without distorting the tractor's frame, which could therefore be of lighter construction.
The Scammell artic went into production in 1921 and was progressively developed up to the 1960s. Another important innovation was the frameless tanker, introduced in 1926. **Illus. 259** and **260** show a box van and a frameless tanker, both dating from 1927. Note that they have four wheels on the trailer axle, although this was by no means universal on Scammells.

258. 1912-15 Knox-Martin Model 31 three-wheeled tractor (USA)

259. 1927 Scammell articulated box van (GB)
260. 1927 Scammell articulated frameless tanker (GB)

261. 1929 Scammell 100-ton articulated low-loader (GB)

Claimed at the time, not without justification, to be the largest lorry in the world, this is the Scammell 100-tonner of 1929, of which only two were built. Despite its great size and carrying capacity, it used the same 7-litre four-cylinder engine as the smaller Scammells, and had a maximum speed of 5-6mph and a fuel consumption of 1 mile per gallon. Both were later fitted with Gardner diesel engines and continued in service until the 1950s. **Illus. 261** shows the Pickford vehicle carrying a diesel-electric locomotive for the Tasmanian Government through St Albans, Hertfordshire, in January 1951. **Illus. 262** shows the steersman's post at the rear of the trailer; his tasks were to steer the rear bogie during difficult turns and to signal to overtaking traffic. Note the telephone for communicating with the driver.

138

262. The rear of the 1929 Scammell

263. 1928 Ford Model AA car transporter (USA)
264. 1935 International articulated logging truck (USA)

During the 1920s most deliveries from factory to dealer were still made by rail, which sometimes involved an awkward journey from the railhead to the showroom. Ford built this early example of a car transporter truck (**illus. 263**), in 1928, based on a six-wheel Model AA chassis. Soon specialized haulaway firms were set up specifically for transporting cars by road. For some time four cars was the maximum load, but with more powerful tractive units and ingenious stowage techniques this has now been raised to thirteen cars.

The articulated truck was of tremendous importance to the logging industry. This 1935 International (**illus. 264**) has a three-axle tractor and two-axle trailer, foreshadowing the multi-wheeler trucks so familiar today. In fact, the tractor is probably a rigid-six truck chassis to which a trailer has been attached without the sophistication of a turntable.

265. 1934 Mack Model CH articulated van (USA)

By the mid-1930s the long-distance articulated truck had acquired many features familiar today. This 1934 Mack Model CH tractor (**illus. 265**) has a sleeper cab and the trailer is fully refrigerated for the carriage of perishable food products between Midwestern cities. The two-axle semi-trailer is another feature that was just coming into use at this time.

A specialized form of articulated vehicle was the mechanical horse, designed to operate in restricted spaces where the horse had reigned supreme because of his small turning circle. An early mechanical horse was the Bulley used in the Chicago stockyards from 1916 onwards, but in Britain the type was developed in response to demand from the railway companies. Karrier built a prototype in 1931, powered by a 7hp flat-twin Jowett engine (**illus. 266**); this was originally intended to be used in conjunction with a horse-drawn trailer as can be seen in the photograph. This was the Karrier Colt; later versions were known as the Cob and had four-cylinder Humber engines and purpose-built trailers. Even more famous than the Karriers were the Scammell mechanical horses. The prototype of these (**illus. 267**) was built by Napier and might well have been continued by this company if it had not decided to concentrate exclusively on aircraft engines. As it was, the whole project was sold to Scammell who put the mechanical horse on the market in 1932. The 3-ton model had a four-cylinder engine of 1125cc capacity, and this was later supplemented by a 6-ton model powered by a 2043cc engine. Both models had four-speed gearboxes. **Illus. 268** shows a 1932 3-ton model on which may be noted some cost-cutting measures such as the single headlamp and doorless cab. The Scammell mechanical horse, including the later Scarab and Townsman developments, was made until 1965.

266. 1931 Karrier prototype mechanical horse (GB)

267. 1931 Napier prototype mechanical horse (GB)

268. 1932 Scammell 3-ton mechanical horse (GB)

FIRE ENGINES

Horse-drawn steam pumpers had been in use for a long time before the appearance of the self-propelled fire engine at the end of the nineteenth century, and some of the latter were simply powered conversions of existing horse-drawn appliances. Such a one was the 1901 Crowden shown in **illus. 269**, fitted with a two-cylinder horizontal steam engine which was provided with steam from the same boiler as the pumping engine. It was one of several built by C. T. Crowden of Leamington Spa, and was owned by the Norwich Union Fire Insurance Company at Worcester.

One of the best-known names in British fire-engine history is that of Merryweather, a company that can trace its origin back to 1690. It built its first self-propelled steam fire engine in 1899, and its first petrol-engined unit in 1903. This was a chemical extinguisher powered by a 24/30hp four-cylinder engine. The 1910 Merryweather in **illus. 270** is towing an auxiliary pumping engine which could be manhandled to a second position at a fire.

A Swedish-made Scania-Vabis ladder and pumping appliance of 1917 (**illus. 271**). It was powered by a comparatively small four-cylinder engine of 2·8 litres, used in the company's 2-ton lorry, a contrast to contemporary American units whose engine capacities could be as high as 15 litres. Tools and hydrant fittings were carried in the running-board lockers. In 1919 Scania-Vabis built a four-wheel-drive fire engine.

A name as famous in the United States as Merryweather in Britain is American La France, a company that has built a wide range of horse-drawn, steam and petrol-engined fire engines since 1903. For a while American La France built two-wheel tractor units that could be coupled to horse-drawn pumpers, but developed at the same time a range of handsome conventional fire engines powered by large six-cylinder engines that could cost as much as $10,000. **Illus. 272** shows a triple combination pumper on a 1921 72hp six-cylinder chassis.

Leyland came into the fire-engine business as a result of a request from the Dublin Fire Brigade in 1909 for an engine on what they considered to be the best commercial chassis made. Leyland's first engine was built to Dublin's specification, but the company subsequently went on to become one of the leading makers in the field. **Illus. 273** is of a combination pumping and ladder truck of 1927. Solid tyres were unusual on fire engines at so late a date.

269. 1901 Crowden two-cylinder steam fire engine (GB)

270. 1910 Merryweather four-cylinder fire engine (GB)

271. 1917 Scania-Vabis four-cylinder 2·8-litre fire engine (S)

272. 1921 American La France 72hp six-cylinder triple combination pumper fire engine (USA)
273. 1927 Leyland four-cylinder combination pumping and ladder-truck fire engine (GB)

An early example of a fire engine on a rigid-six chassis is this 1931 Thornycroft (**illus. 274**), built on a War Office Subsidy-type chassis. By spreading the weight over a greater number of wheels this arrangement made the machine less likely to sink into rough ground, an important consideration when fires had to be reached in remote country areas. The increased length also enabled more equipment to be carried, although on the whole most fire engines have remained four-wheelers up to the present day.

276. 1930 Seagrave articulated ladder truck (USA)

274. 1931 Thornycroft six-wheel fire engine (GB)

275. 1930 Mack Model AC four-cylinder fire engine (USA)

Mack is another well-known name among American fire engines – the company built its first appliance in 1909. A number of fire engines were built on the famous Mack Model AC Bulldog chassis from 1919 to 1930, and the larger six-cylinder AP was also used for fire-engine work. With this, pumping capacity went up to 1000 gallons per minute, compared with 600 gallons from the four-cylinder AC. **Illus. 275** shows a late model AC of about 1930 with twin hose reels.

The articulated ladder truck is a typically American vehicle, few being made anywhere else in the world. The type was built by American La France from about 1914 onwards and was later taken up by most of the major fire-engine manufacturers. Sometimes the trailer axle was steerable, in which case a steersman was perched perilously at the rear of the vehicle. His seat can just be seen on the near side of the trailer of this Seagrave appliance dating from 1930 (**illus. 276**).

278. 1932 Standard Nine fire engine (GB)

277. c. 1923 FIAT 501 fire engine (I)

The smallest fire engines were based on passenger car, or even motorcycle, chassis (see **illus. 367**). **Illus. 277** shows a FIAT 501 of about 1923 with front-mounted pump which seems to be giving quite a respectable jet of water, and **illus. 278** is a British example, a 1932 Standard Nine converted by the National Fire Protection Co Ltd. Despite its small size, it had an engine-driven pump mounted under the seat, three-section extension ladder and a row of chemical extinguishers on each side.

279. 1935 Seagrave V12 combination pumper and ladder truck (USA)

Although the enclosed or 'limousine' fire engine was gaining popularity in the 1930s, the open ladder truck was still being made. These photos show alternative methods of carrying the ladders. **Illus. 279** is a 1935 Seagrave V12 combination pumper and ladder truck with side-mounted extension ladders; the 1939 Hungarian Raba in **illus. 280** carries a turntable ladder. The Raba chassis was made under licence from the German Krupp company; the turntable ladder is also German, by Magirus.

280. 1939 Raba turntable-ladder fire engine (H)
281. 1936 Leyland six-wheel limousine fire engine (GB)

One of the biggest changes in fire-engine
design came during the 1930s with the
appearance of the enclosed or 'limousine'
body. Traditionally, firemen had always
sat along the sides of the vehicle, facing
outwards, but with increasing speeds
numbers of men were thrown off, sometimes
with fatal results. The first security measure
was to place the men inside an open vehicle,
facing inwards, and the next logical step
was to have an all-enclosed body. These
appeared on Dennis and Leyland chassis
in 1931, and were first adopted in America
by Mack in 1935. By the late 1930s they
were widespread in many countries.
Illus. 281 shows a six-wheel Leyland of
1936 specially built for coal-mine work, and
illus. 282 is a Danish Triangel of 1939,
powered by an American six-cylinder
Hercules engine.

282. 1939 Triangel limousine fire engine (DK)

In 1933 American La France adopted a V12
engine for its largest fire engines and in
1937–8 built four remarkable pumpers for
Los Angeles fire brigade, using two V12
engines, one to drive both vehicle and pump,
and the other, behind the driver, solely for
pumping. Known as Metropolitan Duplex
Pumpers, they were the most powerful
pumpers made before World War II. One is
seen here in action in 1952 (**illus. 283**).

283. 1937-8 American La France Metropolitan Duplex Pumper fire engine (USA)

284. 1936 Karrier Bantam 2-ton refuse collector (GB)

MUNICIPAL VEHICLES

Refuse collection has always been the main task of the municipal vehicle and, as in other fields, this was pioneered by Thornycroft with a steam dustcart supplied to Chiswick Vestry in 1897. For a long time the refuse truck remained a fairly simple vehicle, no more than an ordinary sided truck with sliding panels on top to prevent the refuse from blowing about. A typical example of this type is the 1936 Karrier Bantam 2-tonner in **illus. 284**. A somewhat more sophisticated version is shown in **illus. 285**. This is a 1930 Easyloader with separate compartments. Note also the small wheels and solid tyres, a characteristic of a number of municipal vehicles, of which the Shelvoke & Drewry was the best known. Such vehicles gradually displaced the horse in refuse collection work. A further step forward was provided by the moving-floor collector, introduced by the British firm Glover, Webb & Liversidge in 1932. In this, all refuse was fed into the rear of the truck which had a fully enclosed van body.

285. 1930 Easyloader refuse collector (GB)

286. 1932 Scammell mechanical horse with Glover, Webb & Liversidge moving-floor refuse collector trailer (GB)

Illus. 286 shows a body of this type attached to a Scammell mechanical horse of 1932. One solution adopted in other European countries was the barrel body in which refuse was fed either into the sides or rear and crushed before being tipped out. **Illus. 287** shows a German Faun of about 1932 ejecting refuse; in **illus. 288** is a fleet of Swedish Tidaholms, supplied in 1929 to the city of Gothenburg.

288. 1929 Tidaholm refuse collectors (S)

287. c. 1932 Faun refuse collector with tipping barrel body (D)

289. c. 1924 Fowler undertype steam wagon adapted for use as a street sprinkler (GB)

290. 1928 N.A.G. street sprinkler (D)

291. 1933 Bedford six-wheel street sprinkler (GB)

The Fowler undertype steam wagon was in many ways an advanced design, with shaft drive, but its poor steaming abilities earned it a bad reputation and within a few years of its introduction in 1924 it was almost unsaleable as a goods-carrying wagon. However, a number were made as gully emptiers, with a 900-gallon sludge tank from which surplus water could be drained and returned to the drainage system. It could also be used as a street sprinkler, as can be seen in **illus. 289**.

Street sprinkling was another important municipal job, pioneered by the John S. Muir Syndicate of New York who built a steam-driven sweeper/sprinkler in 1903. The N.A.G. in **illus. 290**, dating from 1928, could produce a jet worthy of a fire engine, although it is in fact being used for washing a factory building. Keeping the streets regularly watered is particularly important in tropical countries; the 1933 Bedford six-wheeler in **illus. 291** went to the city of Lourenço Marques, Mozambique.

292. 1902 V.E.C. electric ambulance (USA)

The electric vehicle was an obvious choice for ambulance work because of its silence. This one (**illus. 292**) was built by the Vehicle Equipment Company of Brooklyn in 1902 for the Lying In Hospital of New York City.

Ambulances were built on both passenger-car and commercial-vehicle chassis, the former being the rule in early days when the average commercial chassis was too rough running and slow for the carriage of the sick. In America many ambulances are still based on luxury-car chassis such as Cadillac. In Europe specialized vehicles have been developed, usually using the running gear of light vans. **Illus. 293** shows a very handsome ambulance body on a large Austin chassis of about 1914.

A more utilitarian machine is this 2-ton Bedford ambulance (**illus. 294**), one of four sent to Spain in February 1937 to aid the Republican side in the Civil War. A report by the Spanish Medical Aid Committee praised the Bedfords for their handling, their power on hills and accessibility for greasing.

294. c. 1937 Bedford 2-ton ambulance (GB)

293. c. 1914 Austin 30hp ambulance (GB)

295. *c.* 1900 Riker electric hansom cabs (USA)

TAXICABS

A number of early motor-cab makers
followed the hansom-cab principle, with the
driver perched at the back of the vehicle,
high above his passengers. The Riker
Electric Vehicle Company of Elizabethport,
N.J., made quite a number of electric
hansoms around 1900, which plied for hire
in New York, Chicago, Boston and other
cities. **Illus. 295** shows a fleet of Rikers in
Boston in 1907, by which date they looked
distinctly old-fashioned. The Riker's
passengers were exposed to the elements,
but those who rode in the French Roval
hansom cab of 1909 (**illus. 296**) had the
comforts of a fully enclosed body. The
Roval, which was also made as a light van
steered from the rear, was powered by a
single-cylinder de Dion-Bouton engine.

296. 1909 Roval hansom cab (F)

One of the first petrol-engined cabs to run in London was the Rational (**illus. 297**), made by a small engineering firm in Royston, Hertfordshire. It had a 10/12hp horizontal two-cylinder engine and epicyclic gearbox, and in original form ran on solid tyres, although these were replaced after a year by pneumatics. The London Motor Cab Company ran thirteen Rationals from the summer of 1905 to October 1909.

Despite the efforts of Rational, and other better-known British companies such as Argyll and Wolseley, the majority of London taxicabs up to 1914 were of foreign manufacture, the most popular being French Renaults and Unics. The latter were sold by Mann & Overton who represented Unic until import of the make ceased in 1933, by which time the London company was also selling Austins. Thus it can claim to have sold over 75 per cent of all London's cabs from 1906 to the present. **Illus. 298** shows part of a fleet of Unics in 1908.

297. 1905 Rational 10/12hp two-cylinder taxicab (GB)

298. 1908 Unic 10/12hp two-cylinder taxicabs (F)

One of the few successful specialist makers of taxicabs was Beardmore, a firm that built its first cab in 1919 and its last in 1967. Despite their reputation for heavy steering and difficult operation of clutch and brakes, Beardmores sold in considerable numbers in London and many provincial towns as well. The standard model of the 1920s had a four-cylinder engine of 2409cc and a dropped frame that allowed for a reasonably low entrance, despite the mandatory 10in ground clearance. It was this regulation, one of many laid down by Scotland Yard, that gave London taxis their high and antiquated appearance at a time when passenger cars were becoming lower and longer. The 1923 Beardmore in **illus. 299** has a landaulette body by the little-known Farnham coachbuilder Arnold & Comben.

299. 1923 Beardmore 15hp landaulette taxicab (GB)

300. 1925 FIAT Type 501 landaulette taxicab (I)

FIAT taxis were well known in London up to the early 1920s, and although they were no longer represented in Britain after 1924, Italy's 'universal provider' continued to make cabs, or cars suitable for cab work, right up to the present day. **Illus. 300** shows a 1925 Type 501 landaulette taxi whose driver is taking a call from a cab-rank phone installed on the street corner.

Electricity as a motive power for taxicabs had all but disappeared in Europe by 1914, but it persisted in America, largely thanks to the efforts of the Baker, Rauch & Lang Company of Cleveland, and later Chicopee Falls, Mass., who built electric cabs under the name Raulang until 1928. **Illus. 301** is of a Raulang of about 1924, operated by the Electrotaxi Company of Philadelphia.

301. 1924 Raulang electric taxicab (USA)

In 1927 Scotland Yard's regulations for taxicabs were modified and the 10in ground clearance was reduced to 7in. This encouraged manufacturers to bring out a new generation of cabs that were significantly more modern looking than their predecessors, although still on the high side because of interior headroom requirements. One of the new generation was the Austin; this company had not previously made a cab chassis, but within a few years came to dominate the London cab trade. Introduced in 1930, the Austin cab used the engine from the company's Twelve-Four passenger car; bodies were not supplied by the factory until after World War II, but came from a number of coachbuilding firms such as Strachan who built the three-quarter landaulette shown in **illus. 302**.

302. 1930 Austin Twelve-Four taxicab (GB)

America's leading producer of purpose-built cabs was, and is still, the Checker Cab Manufacturing Company of Kalamazoo, Mich. Founded in 1923, the company built four-cylinder cabs originally, joined by a six in 1927 with a Buda engine, and a Lycoming-powered straight eight in 1932. **Illus. 303** shows a 1940 Model A with six-cylinder Continental engine. Like most of London's cabs made up to World War II, this had a landaulette body, but the open rear quarter looks rather bizarre when combined with the streamlined body shape typical of the American passenger car of the period. Production of the Model A was continued through the war, alongside tank-recovery trailers, Ford truck cabs and an experimental Jeep.

303. 1940 Checker Model A six-cylinder taxicab (USA)

157

BUSES AND TROLLEY BUSES

Thornycroft's undertype steam wagon, introduced in 1897, was soon adapted to passenger-carrying work – an early example was exported to Burma in 1900 and a double-decker was running in London in 1902. The 1901 model in **illus. 305** was used by Marconi for his wireless experiments at Poole, Dorset. The tubular structure lying on the roof was the aerial, which was mounted vertically when in action. Marconi is standing at the rear of the vehicle.

De Dion-Bouton was among the pioneer builders of steam vehicles in France, having made a steam tricycle as early as 1883. From 1894 to 1904 the company manufactured a range of steam buses and lorries that were widely used in metropolitan France and the colonies. Some of these had first- and second-class compartments, although this single-decker of 1901 (**illus. 304**) which operated a service from Septeuil to Vétheuil was a one-class bus.

Another well-known French builder of steam vehicles was Valentin Purrey of Bordeaux who made goods and

304. 1901 de Dion-Bouton single-decker steam bus (F)
305. 1901 Thornycroft steam bus (GB)

passenger-carrying undertypes from 1902 to 1913. **Illus. 306** shows a 'train' consisting of bus and two two-wheeled trailers in which, it was claimed, 110 men were carried across snow, though the distance covered was not stated. It was taken at the artillery barracks at Bordeaux on 24 January 1907.

The first regular motor-bus service in London was operated in 1899, and from then until the introduction of the B type in 1910, which soon came to dominate the fleets, a wide variety of makes and motive powers was tried. Some were operated by existing horse-bus companies, such as the London General Omnibus Company and the London Road Car Company. Among the new concerns specially formed to operate motor buses, the best known was the London Motor Omnibus Company whose fleet name was Vanguard. These photos show just a few of the vehicles involved in this experimental period. **Illus. 307** is one of a fleet of twenty-six Clarkson steam buses which the Road Car Company put into service in 1905. They had a good turn of speed, but boiler maintenance proved expensive and they were withdrawn during 1907.

14⁵ d'Artillerie. Quartier Nansouty_Bordeaux   24 Janvier 1907   Transport sur la neige de 110 hommes par train Purrey

306. 1906 Valentin Purrey steam bus with two two-wheeled trailers (F)

307. c. 1905 Clarkson steam bus (GB)

308. 1906 Straker-Squire petrol-engined double-decker bus (GB)
309. 1907 Electrobus battery-driven double-decker bus (GB)

Illus. 308 is a petrol-engined bus, a
Straker-Squire of 1906. This make, which
was based on the German Büssing, was at
one time the most popular in London, and
356 were running in 1908 operated by
several different firms. In **illus. 309** is shown
a battery-electric bus, of which a small
fleet was operated by the London
Electrobus Company from July 1907 to
March 1910 when they were sold to
Brighton, where they continued to run
until 1916. Their smoothness and silence
was much appreciated, but the weight of
their batteries restricted their speed.

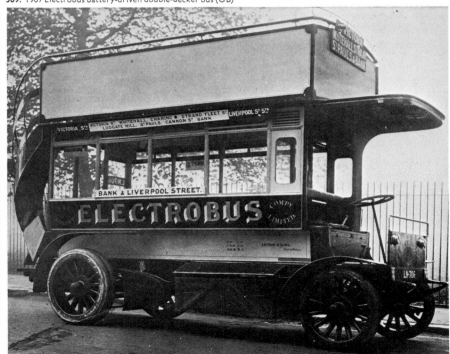

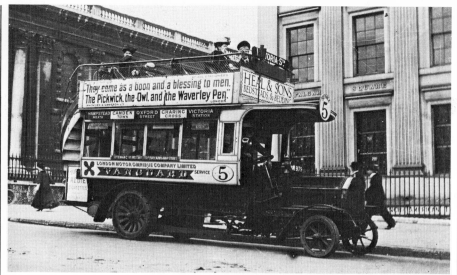

The most popular make after Straker-Squire is shown in **illus. 310**; it is a 1908 Milnes-Daimler operated by Vanguard which in that year merged with London General and Road Car Companies to form a greatly enlarged London General. It was this company that set about designing and building a new bus, the X type, prototype of the B type. The latter became the standard London bus and over 2900 were built.

Like London, Paris had a wide variety of buses until she standardized on Brillié-Schneider and Renault in the 1920s. One of the more unusual vehicles was this 1905 Kriéger petrol-electric double-decker (**illus. 311**), in which a petrol engine generated electricity for two electric motors which drove the rear wheels.

Double-deckers had disappeared from Paris by 1914, not to be seen again until the 1960s.

310. 1908 Milnes-Daimler petrol-engined double-decker bus (D/GB)
311. 1905 Kriéger petrol-electric double-decker bus (F)

Before building its own buses, the Fifth Avenue Coach Company of New York used a large number of de Dion-Bouton buses, as well as some British Daimlers. **Illus. 312** shows a de Dion-Bouton of 1913 experimentally fitted with petrol-electric drive; about ten such de Dions had been built in 1908, but this one, number 160, was the last and only ran for a few years. In 1916 the first bus to come from Fifth Avenue's own workshops was made, and from 1917 to 1921, 240 double-deckers of this type were built. They had Knight sleeve-valve engines built by Root & Vandervoort under licence from British Daimler and originally carried forty-seven passengers, later increased to fifty-one. **Illus. 313** shows one of this series on Fifth Avenue in 1921. Note the absence of mudguards, which were not standardized until after 1925. Closed-top double-deckers came to New York in 1922.

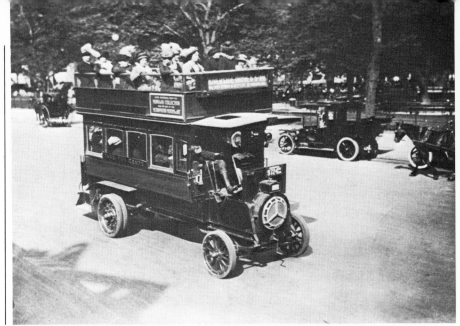

312. 1913 de Dion-Bouton petrol-electric double-decker bus (F)

313. 1917-21 Fifth Avenue Coach Company double-decker bus (USA)

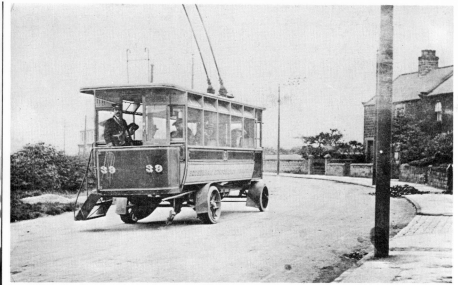

The trolley bus first appeared in Germany at the turn of the century and came to Britain in 1909 when experiments were made in London with a single-decker by Metropolitan Electric Tramways Ltd. This vehicle never went into service, and it was in Yorkshire that the trolley system was first used commercially. Leeds opened two trolley-bus routes on 20 June 1911, and Bradford followed four days later. The next cities to turn to trolleys were Rotherham (October 1912), Stockport (March 1913) and Keighley (April 1913). **Illus. 314** shows a Straker-Clough single-decker on a semi-rural route at Rotherham. These early trolley buses were odd-looking vehicles, with little bonnets ahead of the driver and, frequently, open-fronted cabs. Full fronts did not come until after World War I, as on the 1923 Wolverhampton-operated Tilling Stevens thirty-six-seater in **illus. 315**.

314. 1912 Straker-Clough single-decker trolley bus (GB)

315. 1923 Tilling Stevens single-decker trolley bus (GB)

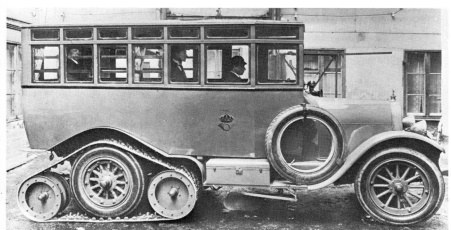

Many rural bus services also carried the mail, some buses having a small mailbox into which letters could be dropped at each stop. In some countries such as Switzerland and Sweden bus services were, and are, operated by the postal authorities. **Illus. 316** is of a 1923 Scania-Vabis postal bus (note the crown and posthorn on the side) with snowtracks. In addition to the tracks it carries a small snowplough below the running board.

316. 1923 Scania-Vabis postal bus (S)

163

317. 1928 Fageol Twin Coach thirty-seven passenger bus (USA)

One of the most significant steps in bus design was taken by the brothers Frank and William Fageol who formed the Twin Coach Company in 1927, building a single-decker bus with two six-cylinder 55bhp engines mounted under seats behind the front axle. The total length of the vehicle could be used for passenger carrying, entrance and exit doors being ahead of the front, and behind the rear axles. This layout was soon copied by most other bus makers, and although the twin engines have not survived, the modern bus has not changed greatly in appearance from this 1928 model, certainly much less than have trucks or passenger cars.
Illus. 317 shows a thirty-seven-passenger 'suburban express' bus built for the Central Transportation Company of Trenton, N.J.

319. 1927 Guy rigid-six double-decker bus (GB)

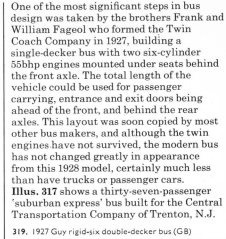

318. c. 1926 Büssing rigid-six bus (D)

The rigid-six layout became popular for passenger vehicles a few years after it first appeared on trucks, and was widely adopted in countries such as Britain where there was a legal restriction on the length of a two-axle vehicle. The German Büssing company made a wide variety of six-wheelers, of which an early example is shown in **illus. 318**. This dates from about 1926 and is light enough to require only single wheels on the rear axles; Büssing also built enormous eighty-one-passenger double-deckers for Berlin with twin wheels on each axle, and, in 1934, a twelve-cylinder 27-litre three-axle single-decker with a maximum speed of nearly 60mph.
Illus. 319 shows an early British rigid-six double-decker, a 1927 Guy operated by the London Public Omnibus Company Ltd, one of the so-called pirate companies that vied with the London General in the 1920s. Public operated fourteen of these sixty-seater Guys, which were the first six-wheeler buses to run on London streets.

320. *c.* 1928 Six Wheel Company (Safeway) double-decker bus (USA)

The Six Wheel Company of Philadelphia was formed with the express purpose of manufacturing rigid-six buses, both single- and double-deckers, although a few trucks were made as well. The six-cylinder engines were made by Continental, and the tandem rear axle suspension arrangement was used by Six Wheel under licence from Goodyear Tire & Rubber Company who had pioneered this type of vehicle. Sizeable fleets of Six Wheel buses ran in New York, Detroit, Cleveland, Akron and Kansas City, as well as in smaller towns, during their heyday, 1924 to 1928. **Illus. 320** shows one of twenty-seven operated by the Surface Transportation Corp. of New York in 1928. The body is by Fitzgibbon & Crisp of Trenton, N.J.

Dennis had been a popular make with the independent London bus operators of the 1920s, and in 1930 the company introduced the Lance (**illus. 321**), a modern double-decker chassis to compete with A.E.C.'s Regent and Leyland's Titan. Some were bought by independents, but the London General also ordered a fleet of twenty-five, to be operated in the livery of a subsidiary, Overground Ltd. They had metal-framed bodies by Metropolitan Cammell, in contrast to the composite-framed bodies of the A.E.C.s that formed the bulk of the General fleet. When London Transport came into being in 1933 the Lances lost their Overground livery and were sold in 1937.

321. 1930 Dennis Lance double-decker buses (GB)

Perhaps the best-known London bus of the inter-war period was the STL made for London Transport by A.E.C. at Southall, with bodies mainly coming from London Transport's own works at Chiswick. Like its predecessor, the ST, the STL was based on A.E.C.'s Regent chassis, but was 8½in longer, hence the 'L' suffix (long ST). Introduced in 1933, they had seating for sixty passengers, making them the largest vehicles yet built for London on a two-axle chassis, although later models had

322. 1935-6 A.E.C. Model STL fifty-six-seater London bus (GB)

323. 1935 A.E.C. Model STL with full-front cab (GB)

fifty-six-seater bodies. Up to 1938 a six-cylinder petrol engine was used, but this was then replaced by a diesel unit, which was employed on all STLs until production ceased in 1946. A total of 2649 STLs were built. **Illus. 322** shows one of a batch of 500 made in 1935–6 with fifty-six-seater Chiswick bodies; **illus. 323** is of an experimental full-fronted STL of 1935, later fitted with a normal half-cab.

The first British maker to follow Twin Coach's lead in moving the engine from the traditional position at the front of the chassis was A.E.C., who introduced the Q type in 1932. In this the engine was mounted on the off side, just behind the front axle, enabling forty-seater single-deck, and sixty-three-seater double-deck bodies to be employed. Only five double-decker Qs were built, four

324. 1934 A.E.C. Q type double-decker bus (GB)

two-axle models and one with three axles, but a total of 233 single-deckers were supplied to London Transport between 1932 and 1936. Lack of acceptance from operators generally at that time led to the discontinuance of the design. **Illus. 324** shows the first of the double-decker Qs, built in 1934; in **illus. 325** is a 1936 single-decker with thirty-seven-seater Park Royal body. These served until 1953.

325. 1936 A.E.C. Q type single-decker bus (GB)

The rear-engined double-decker reached
New York streets in 1936 when the Fifth
Avenue Coach Company bought a fleet of
seventy-one passenger buses with
transverse rear engines built by the Yellow
Coach Company. New York took 160 in all,
and Chicago 140. All were one-man
operated, and some were later converted to
diesel engines. The last ones were retired
from Chicago service in 1950, and from New
York in 1953. **Illus. 326** shows a Model 735
on Riverside Drive Viaduct in 1948.

326. 1936 Yellow Coach Company Model 735 rear-engined double-decker bus (USA)

327. 1938-40 Twin Coach experimental 'Super Twin' trolley bus (USA)

Twin Coach built four experimental 'Super Twins' between 1938 and 1940, three motor buses and one trolley bus (**illus. 327**). With three axles evenly spaced along the chassis, they could seat fifty-eight passengers, but although front and rear axles steered, as can be seen in the photograph, they were not articulated, as some European three-axle buses are. However, the central joint was constructed so that the two halves of the bus could respond to road shocks and changes in grade. The photograph shows the trolley bus as a demonstrator in 1940; it was sold to Cleveland Transit System in 1942.

CHARABANCS, TOURING AND LONG-DISTANCE COACHES

A popular vehicle from which to see the sights of New York was the 'rubberneck' bus which was widely used in the years up to 1914. As in most early charabancs the seats are arranged in tiers to give rear-seat passengers a good view forwards. Since even the front seats are rather high from the ground, ladders must have been provided at the beginning and end of each journey. Many of the rubberneck buses were electric, as is the one in **illus. 328** which dates from about 1906.

The charabanc dates back to the horse-drawn era, and almost as soon as motorized vehicles were developed they began to be used for pleasure excursions. Britain's first recorded charabanc journey was from London to Clacton on Sea in 1898, operated by a Daimler seven-seater. By 1906, the date of these two photographs, charabanc excursions were a regular summer feature of holiday resorts

328. c. 1906 'rubberneck' electric charabanc (USA)

throughout Europe, although they were not usually operated from the big cities as later. The railways took passengers to the resorts, from which the 'charas' operated day trips.

Illus. 329 shows a Milnes-Daimler owned by the Great Western Railway, and **illus. 330** (overleaf) an Albion with a 12hp two-cylinder engine in Ireland.

329. 1906 Milnes-Daimler four-cylinder charabanc (D/GB)

330. 1906 Albion 12hp two-cylinder charabanc (GB)

Not strictly a charabanc, but doubtless used for staff pleasure outings, is this 1913 Daimler estate bus photographed outside Palace House, Beaulieu (**illus. 331**). The little 1903 de Dion-Bouton next to it survived to become the first exhibit in the Montagu Motor Museum, but the Daimler, alas, is no longer known to exist.

During the 1920s the Pickwick Stages System rebuilt commercial chassis to suit its own needs, and followed this by assembly of its own designs in the company workshops. The most remarkable of these was the sleeper coach 'Alsacia', completed in 1928 (**illus. 334**). This was of chassisless all-metal construction, and contained thirteen two-berth compartments, plus a lavatory. Only one was built, but four others of modified design went into service between Los Angeles and San Francisco.

331. 1913 Daimler 40hp estate bus (GB) with a 1903 6hp de Dion-Bouton (F)

332. 1922 Daimler charabanc (GB)

The Parlour Coach was a very popular American vehicle in the 1920s. Considering their size they did not carry many passengers, but they were extremely comfortable, and a powerful engine made for high speeds on inter-city services. By 1925 there were 6500 bus operators, many of them running coaches similar to the White in **illus. 333**. As mergers gradually took place, so a national network of coach operation grew, leading by the late 1930s to the nationwide service offered by Greyhound and other famous companies.

The early 1920s was the golden age of the open charabanc, which by this time was not restricted to the resorts, but regularly sallied forth from the big cities to the seaside, often giving the poorer members of the population their only chance to escape from bricks and smoke. Many of them were run by ex-Servicemen who spent their demobilization gratuities on a charabanc or two, sometimes built on an ex-Army chassis. This 1922 Daimler (**illus. 332**), is typical of the period; seats are no longer ranged in tiers, and there are doors to each row of seats. A small ladder is carried above the running board.

333. *c.* 1927 White six-cylinder Parlour Coach (USA)

334. 1928 Pickwick Stages System 'Alsacia' sleeper coach (USA)

335. 1936 Ford V8 eleven-seater bus (USA)

336. 1929 London-Watford coach (GB)

Some medium-distance bus services were operated in the 1930s by lengthened versions of passenger cars, such as the 1936 Ford V8 in **illus. 335** which could carry eleven passengers in addition to the driver. Today such vehicles are normally only used for hotel or airport work, although a Checker Aerobus was used briefly in the 1960s in England for a high-speed service from London to Bristol.

In Britain too, long-distance coaching became widespread and much more comfortable in the late 1920s, particularly with the introduction of the dropped frame which allowed easier entrance and gave a lower centre of gravity. Light refreshments were served on some coaches, which might also carry a cigarette machine, clock, barometer and flower vases. The coach in **illus. 336** operated the London-Watford service and is shown setting down passengers in London's Regent Street.

The building of Germany's *Autobahn* network encouraged the development of streamlined coaches capable of higher speeds than any elsewhere in the world. On runs between cities such as Frankfurt and Munich they averaged 50mph; this included negotiating city traffic at each end of the journey, so they had to be capable of 70mph on the *Autobahn*. The photos show (**illus. 337**) two Henschels of about 1935, and (**illus. 338**) a 1938 Mercedes-Benz. All were operated by the state organization, Deutsche Reichsbahn.

337. 1935 Henschel streamlined *Autobahn* coaches (D)

338. 1938 Mercedes-Benz *Autobahn* coach (D)
339. 1936 Yellow Coach Company Model 719 thirty-seven-seater coach (USA)

The first of the 'Super Coaches' built by Yellow Coach Company, a General Motors subsidiary, for Pacific Greyhound Lines went into service in 1936. With seating capacity for thirty-seven passengers, they were powered by a 707ci petrol engine mounted transversely at the rear and had fully enclosed underfloor luggage compartments. A total of 329 were built in 1936 (Model 719), followed by 1256 of the similar-looking Model 743, made from 1937 to 1939. Some of the 1939 Model 743s had Detroit Diesel engines. They were succeeded by the more modern-looking Model 744 which was made until well after World War II. **Illus. 339** shows a Model 719 in the 'Big Sur' country of California, taken in 1936.

MOTORCYCLES AND MOTOR TRICYCLES

INTRODUCTION

In theory at any rate the motorcycle has a history considerably longer than that of the automobile. The foot-propelled hobby horse was around in some numbers by the second decade of the nineteenth century, and as steam power was being employed for railway locomotives and boats as well as for a few experimental road vehicles, it was to be expected that someone would suggest applying steam to the hobby horse. The resulting vehicle was christened *Velocipedraisiavaporianna* (steam-driven velocipede), and was illustrated in cartoon form in 1818. As there were no technical details to show how the steam engine was linked to the wheels it is more than likely that this machine was never built. With the growth of steam road carriages, especially in England, it is quite possible that some steam-driven two-wheelers were made between the 1820s and 1860s, but no records have survived.

The first motorcycle that is known to have run was the French Michaux-Perraux of 1869. This used the frame of the Michaux 'boneshaker', a commercially built pedal-driven velocipede, powered by a Perreaux single-cylinder steam engine which drove the rear wheel by means of a pulley and flexible belt. It was too much of a novelty to have any commercial success, nor did the various steam tricycles made in England in the 1870s and 1880s find any buyers. However, an American inventor, Lucius Copeland, built a steam-powered Ordinary bicycle in 1883, and followed this with a series of tricycles, some of which were built by the Northrup Manufacturing Company of Camden, N.J. He fixed a price of $500 for these and sold a few, but he made little profit at this figure and noted with regret ' . . . people will not pay more than $500 for a motor vehicle'.

It was the internal-combustion engine that first made the motorcycle a viable proposition, and even then it was some years before many were built. Daimler's machine of 1885 may have been the first petrol-engined cycle, but it never went into production, and even the motorcycles of Hildebrand & Wolfmüller and Holden were made only in limited numbers. The true ancestor of the modern motorcycle was the 1901 Werner which had its engine mounted integrally with the frame, instead of being attached to it in the manner of the contemporary Minerva or Clément which were no more than powered bicycles. These early machines had single-cylinder engines, but as with cars, designers found that there was a limit to the process of increasing power by enlarging the cylinder, and the only solution was to proceed to two cylinders. The 90° V-twin was the obvious choice, for it fitted conveniently into the diamond-shaped frame between the front and rear wheels. In Britain, J. A. Prestwich of London was the pioneer of the V-twin layout, supplying engines to many motorcycle makers as well as to quite a number of light-car firms, especially during the cyclecar boom of 1912–15. In France, Clément, Griffon and Peugeot were among the earlier firms to take up the V-twin, and in the United States, Indian and Harley-Davidson.

Two alternative designs of two-cylinder engine were the vertical twin, and the flat, or horizontally opposed, twin. The former was a rarity on motorcycles until the 1930s, but the flat twin was popular, in particular with the British Douglas company who made machines almost exclusively of this layout until 1957. The four-cylinder engine was never widely used in two-wheelers, although the Belgian F.N. company made a shaft-drive four from 1905 to 1923, and in their early days they were no more expensive than simpler machines. Other firms to make inline fours included the Austrian Laurin & Klement, the German Dürkopp and the American Henderson.

The motor tricycle was originally a powered version of the pedal tricycle, with cycle-type single front wheel and two rear wheels driven by a single-cylinder engine without benefit of clutch or gearbox. The most popular of these was the de Dion-Bouton, made in large numbers from 1895 to 1901, but by this time a new form of three-wheeler was making its appearance, the tricar or forecar. In this the axle and two wheels were at the front, and between them was mounted a passenger seat, originally a very light wickerwork affair, but with the coming of two-cylinder engines and increased power, the seat became a proper coachbuilt one. Gradually the tricar took on more of the features of the motorcar, a seat replaced the rider's saddle, handlebars gave way to wheel steering, and watercooled engines necessitated a radiator. The last of these carlike tricars were made in 1908, after which the sociable advantages of side-by-side seating and better weather protection persuaded the public that the light car was a better proposition.

One feature that was quite lacking on the early motorcycles was any form of clutch or gear-change mechanism. Starting was effected by pushing the machine along and vaulting into the saddle when the engine coughed into life. But with increasing size and weight, especially when the newly popular sidecar was employed, it became essential to vary speeds, and numerous systems came into use, of which the variable pulley and belt, and the epicyclic hub gear were the most common. N.S.U. marketed a simple epicyclic belt pulley that could be added to a single-speed motorcycle. Later and more elaborate forms of adjustable-pulley gear change were the Zenith Gradua of 1909 and the Rudge Multi of 1911. These were, of course, used with belt drive, but by 1912 chain drive was increasingly establishing itself, especially with multi-cylinder engines. At about this time the oilbath chaincase came in, which completely protected the chain and kept it continuously lubricated.

When war broke out in 1914, a large number of second-hand motorcycles were bought by the War Office for dispatch work, but later two makes were standardized, the 550cc single-cylinder Triumph and the 350cc flat-twin Douglas. The dispatch riders performed an essential task, for wireless communication was not widely available, and their rides on atrocious roads pitted with shell holes have entered the legends of 1914–18. Like the Thornycroft lorry, the Douglas motorcycle gained tremendous prestige from the war which was to help sales in the 1920s.

Just after the war there was a brief vogue for the motor scooter which in its simplest form had no seat. Some scooters on the other hand, such as the Unibus, provided more weather protection than the ordinary motorcycle, and were aimed especially at the feminine market. However, their low speed (20–25mph) and the relative cheapness of a proper motorcycle prevented their widespread acceptance, and by the mid-1920s they had disappeared both in Europe and the United States.

Two developments of the 1920s were the increasing use of the pillion seat and of the sidecar. Before 1914 most female pillion riders had sat side-saddle as they did on horseback, and on a cushion strapped to the carrier rather than a proper seat. This uncomfortable and dangerous practice was eliminated in the 1920s by a greater willingness to sit astride the saddle, and by purpose-built, sprung pillion seats. With greater power available the sidecar could become more elaborate and some very handsome coachbuilt examples appeared, especially from the pioneer firm of Mills & Fulford. The family man could now take his wife and three children, if they were small enough; wife and two toddlers in the sidecar, and an older child on the pillion seat. Even a 750cc motorcycle with sidecar was cheaper to buy and run than a small car, and particularly after the Depression of 1929–31 the motorcycle combination was the recognized holiday transport of thousands of more prosperous working men. (The poorly paid worker could still afford no personal transport other than a bicycle at best.) The commercial sidecar had long been used for deliveries and the carriage of samples, but a new use for it in the 1920s was as a taxi. Although Scotland Yard regulations prevented any of these from running in London, they were a feature of a number of provincial cities in Britain, including Glasgow, Nottingham, Birmingham, Margate and Brighton. Using powerful motorcycles by B.S.A., Campion and other makers, they could seat two passengers side by side, or in staggered position. In Berlin a large fleet of sidecar taxis ran up to the end of the 1920s, and in Vienna there were three-wheelers with the front portion of a motorcycle and a two-wheeled rickshaw-type body behind.

Technically the 1920s were a period of consolidation rather than striking innovation, certainly among the designs that achieved commercial success. The vertical single-cylinder continued to be popular for sizes up to 500cc, two variations being the Barr & Stroud single sleeve-valve unit and the Bradshaw oilcooled engine, the latter used in two-cylinder form in the Belsize-Bradshaw light car. Despite the success of the flat-twin Douglas, and later the B.M.W., the classic motorcycle engine was the V-twin, made in sizes up to 1000cc and with increasing use of ohv. The inline four was continued by F.N. until 1923, and in America the Henderson company made its 1168cc aircooled four up to 1931. Other American four-cylinder machines were the 600cc Cleveland and the 1229cc A.C.E., the latter taken over by Indian and sold as the Indian Ace until 1929. Two-stroke engines were used in a variety of light motorcycles such as Levis, Dunelt and Velocette; Scott's two-stroke Squirrel and Super Squirrel were made throughout the inter-war period.

In 1935 Triumph introduced its 650cc vertical twin, reviving a layout that had been dormant since about 1907. Fours were also coming back into favour, not the inline variety but the square four with two parallel rows of two cylinders, or the Matchless narrow-angle V4. George Brough, whose Brough Superior was often called the Rolls-Royce of motorcycles, introduced his Golden Dream in 1938; this had a 997cc four-cylinder engine made up of two superimposed flat twins. Final drive was by shaft and three- or four-speed gearboxes could be had. Unfortunately only six were made, all to special order, before World War II intervened. The price was fixed at £185.

In America the motorcycle was being used increasingly for police work, and the large four-cylinder Indian or the Harley-Davidson V-twin were the most popular mounts. In 1940 the Los Angeles Police Motor Squad had the largest fleet of motorcycles in the world, including over 100 three-wheeler Harley-Davidsons for traffic-control work.

341. 1896 Hildebrand & Wolfmüller two-cylinder motorcycle (D)

In 1894 three German engineers, Heinrich and Wilhelm Hildebrand and Alois Wolfmüller, put a motorcycle into production which sold in reasonable quantities until 1898 (**illus. 341**). The engine was a watercooled flat twin of 1487cc capacity whose pistons were connected by external rods to two parallel cranks on the rear axle. Maximum speed was about 28mph. The makers were the first to use the word *Motorrad* (literally, motor wheel) for a powered two-wheeler, and actually patented the name, but after they left the motor industry it came to be used in German-speaking countries for all motorcycles.

The first petrol-engined motorcycle in the world was built by Gottlieb Daimler in 1885–6, and first ridden by his assistant Wilhelm Maybach in November 1886. Like Daimler's first car of the same date, it used a vertical single-cylinder engine with hot-tube ignition. Drive was by belt to a countershaft which connected with an internally toothed gear ring on the rear wheel. The wooden frame seems very heavy and doubtless Maybach was glad of the small stabilizing wheels. The two inventors soon concentrated on four wheels and neither the Daimler company nor its successor, Daimler-Benz, has ever made another motorcycle. **Illus. 340** shows a replica as the original was destroyed by fire.

342. 1896 Pennington two-cylinder tandem motorcycle (GB)

One of the most colourful figures on the early motoring scene was the American, Edward Joel Pennington, who designed, and had built for him in various factories on both sides of the Atlantic, a wide variety of two-, three-, and four-wheeled vehicles. His motorcycle (**illus. 342**), of which only two were made, in the Humber works at Coventry in 1896, had a horizontal two-cylinder engine mounted behind the rear wheel, driving directly via cranks on the rear wheel hub. The plain steel barrel cylinders had no cooling at all, and the whole design was dubious in the extreme, yet the financier H. J. Lawson parted with more than £100,000 for the British rights. A widely publicized Pennington advertisement showed one of his motorcycles leaping over a river, Evel Knievel fashion.

340. 1885-6 Daimler single-cylinder motorcycle (D)

343. 1897 Holden four-cylinder motorcycle (GB)
344. 1900 de Dion-Bouton motor tricycle (F)

Illus. 343 shows the first motorcycle of British design and manufacture, built by Colonel H. C. Holden in 1897. It was unusual in having a horizontally opposed four-cylinder engine at a time when four-cylinder cars were extremely rare. A small number were produced in a factory at Kennington, South East London, from 1898 to 1903. The basketwork two-wheeled trailer was not a standard fitment.

The de Dion-Bouton tricycle pioneered the high-speed engine, which ran at up to 1500rpm, at which speed the 137cc unit developed about $\frac{3}{4}$hp. The first tricycles were made in 1895, and in the following year the capacity was increased to 250cc. With various sizes of engine the de Dion tricycles were raced with great success and large numbers were made up to 1901, including licence manufacture in Britain, Belgium, Germany and America. **Illus. 344** shows a 1900 model with what were optimistically called 'puncture preventers' behind the rear wheels.

In 1900 Messrs Perks & Birch of Coventry, Warwickshire, introduced their motor wheel, designed to be fitted in place of the rear wheel of a pedal cycle. The Singer company took up the motor wheel, mounting it at the front of its tricycle. It was sold under the name Compact. In 1901 Singer announced the Trivoiturette which could be had either with a rear-facing basketwork seat for a passenger, or, as shown in **illus. 345**, with a carrier for loads of up to 200lb. The rider is Edwin Perks, designer of the motor wheel.

With proprietary engines widely available, many early motorcyclists built their own machines. An example from the English Midlands is Mr Milbrowe Smith of Handsworth Wood, Birmingham, seen on the machine he built in 1902 (**illus. 346**). It was powered by a single-cylinder 1½hp Minerva engine and had belt drive, a Sturmey-Archer back-pedal brake and Brooks saddle. Its weight was 120lb. Milbrowe Smith was a founder member of the Birmingham Motor Cycle Club.

The Quadrant Works of Birmingham was well known for motorcycles and tricars. Early models of 1901–3 had single-cylinder 211cc Minerva engines, but later the firm made its own power units, in a variety of sizes including a very large single of 780cc and V-twins of 1130cc. **Illus. 347** shows a belt-driven single of 1902 known as the Quadrant Autocyclette, with the well-known motoring writer Sir Max Pemberton.

345. 1901 Singer Trivoiturette with attached carrier (GB)
346. 1902 Milbrowe Smith motorcycle powered by a single-cylinder 1½hp Minerva engine   **347.** 1902 Quadrant Autocyclette powered by a single-cylinder 211cc Minerva engine

348. 1904 Phoenix Trimo 3½hp tricar (GB)
349. c. 1904 Rex tricar (GB)

An early development of the motorcycle was the tricar in which the front wheel was replaced by a pair of wheels mounted on a light axle. Originally developed to improve handling and reduce the danger of skidding in winter, it was an obvious step to fill the space between the front wheels by a basketwork seat for a passenger. Although the first tricars were converted from two-wheelers, it was soon found that a more substantial frame was necessary, and the best tricars were built as such. Among the most popular in England was the Phoenix Trimo, introduced in 1902 with a 2hp clip-on engine which was replaced in 1904 by a 3½hp integrally mounted engine. This 1904 improved Trimo (illus. 348) had a clutch and two-speed epicyclic gear, features not normally found on motorcycles until a few years later. Another popular British tricar was the Birmingham-built Rex (illus. 349). Gradually the tricar took on more features of the motorcar: the rider's saddle was replaced by a seat, handlebars gave way to a steering wheel, and watercooled engines with car-type radiators made their

appearance by 1906. An early example of a driver's seat was seen on the Century Tandem (**illus. 350**), which was made almost unchanged from 1899 to 1904. Engines were by de Dion-Bouton, Aster, or M.M.C. Tricars were equally popular in France and **illus. 351** shows a 'Concours de Tricars' of 1905 with two of the vehicles awaiting weighing-in before the start. Among the better-known French makes were Werner and Contal; the makers of the latter were courageous enough to enter one of their machines in the 11,000-mile Peking-Paris Race of 1907, but alas it was abandoned in the Gobi Desert.

350. 1900-4 Century Tandem tricar (GB)
351. Before the start of a 'Concours de Tricars' in France, 1905

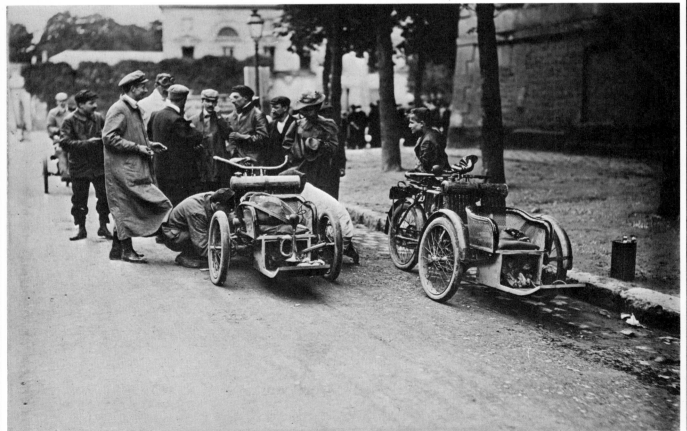

Another way of carrying a passenger was provided by the trailer, of which this elegant canework model is a typical example (**illus. 352**). Trailers were very light but less comfortable than might appear from the posed photograph, for the passenger was exposed not only to mud thrown up by the motorcycle, but also to its exhaust fumes. A much more practical solution was the sidecar, which was used from 1903 onwards.

Although a few vertical twins were made by Werner and other manufacturers, the classic two-cylinder motorcycle engine was the V-twin which fitted so logically into the diamond frame. This layout appeared in 1905; among the best-known makers were the British J.A.P. who mainly made engines for other people, the French Peugeot, Clément and Griffon, and the American Harley-Davidson and Indian. **Illus. 353** shows an Indian 4hp at a check in Herefordshire during the 1907 Auto Cycle Club 1000 Miles Trial. The rider (with armband) is Teddy Hastings who travelled over from America specially for the trial.

352. *c.* 1903 motorcycle with trailer (GB)
353. 1907 Indian 4hp V-twin motorcycle (USA)

354. 1911 Indian V-twin motorcycle (USA)
355. c. 1914 Douglas belt-driven horizontally opposed flat-twin motorcycle with sidecar (GB)

In 1908 Indian introduced a torpedolike petrol tank carried on the top frame tube instead of behind the rider, and this location for the tank, although not necessarily the torpedo shape, was soon adopted by many makers. **Illus. 354** shows a 1911 Indian V-twin at Brooklands, with C. B. Franklin in the saddle.

An alternative to the V-twin was the horizontally opposed flat-twin, of which the best-known exponent was Douglas Motors Ltd of Bristol. This company adopted in 1907 the flat-twin engine designed by J. F. Barter and never used any other engine layout, except for a short-lived and unimportant single-cylinder in the 1930s. The most popular engine sizes were 350, 500 and 600cc. **Illus. 355** is a belt-drive Douglas with sidecar, dating from about 1914.

The Rudge-Whitworth company had been well known in the pedal-cycle world since the 1880s, and in 1911 it turned to the manufacture of motorcycles. The most distinctive feature of Rudge-Whitworth machines was the Multi variable-pulley gear which gave two speeds at a time when the majority of motorcycles were restricted to a single speed. Another adjustable-pulley gear was the Zenith Gradua, but both these systems put a great strain on the belts, and in the 1920s they were replaced by three- or four-speed all-chain transmissions. **Illus. 356** shows a Rudge Multi of about 1914.

Four-cylinder motorcycles have never been widespread, but one of the best known, and the longest lived, was the Henderson from Rochester, N.Y. (later Detroit, Cleveland, and Chicago). Designed by Bill Henderson, the original 1911 model had four separate aircooled cylinders with overhead inlet valves, and a capacity of 1068cc. A most unusual optional extra was a reverse gear. Later Henderson fours had side-valve engines with capacities of 1168 and 1301cc. **Illus. 357** is of a 1914 model with a substantial sidecar.

356. c. 1914 Rudge-Whitworth Multi motorcycle (GB)
357. 1914 Henderson four-cylinder motorcycle with sidecar (USA)

358. 1916 Autoped 155cc single-cylinder scooter (USA)

359. 1920-2 Unibus 269cc scooters (GB)

360. 1926 Ro-Monocar 250cc scooter (GB)

361. 1920 A.B.C. Skootamota 125cc scooter (GB)

Immediately after World War I there was quite a vogue for motor scooters, although none achieved the phenomenal success of their later counterparts, the Vespa and Lambretta. **Illus. 358** shows one of the earliest, an American-built Autoped of 1916 powered by a 155cc single-cylinder engine mounted on, and driving, the front wheel. The hinged steering column controlled clutch, throttle and brake, and the rider had to stand for whatever length of journey he chose to endure. Rather more civilized was the A.B.C. Skootamota (**illus. 361**) which had a seat and conventional braking. Power came from a 125cc engine mounted over the rear wheel. The Skootamota was advertised as particularly suitable for ladies, often being photographed with District Nurses. Another scooter was the Unibus, made by the Gloucestershire Aircraft Co Ltd of Cheltenham from 1920 to 1922. Powered by a 269cc two-stroke engine, the Unibus had an enclosed streamlined body and car-type pressed-steel chassis. **Illus. 359** shows two Unibuses sharing a showroom with an Albert car. A further refinement of the scooter principle was the Ro-Monocar (**illus. 360**) designed by the aviation pioneer, Sir Alliott Verdon-Roe, maker of Avro aircraft. This had a car-type seat, and the 250cc Villiers two-stroke engine drove via a three-speed gearbox and shaft-and-worm final drive. Verdon-Roe made extensive personal use of his Ro-Monocar, but it was never built for sale.

362. *c.* 1920 A.J.S. motorcycle with single-seater sidecar (GB)

363. *c.* 1923 B.S.A. 770cc V-twin motorcycle with sidecar (GB)

From modest beginnings as a light canework structure in 1903, the sidecar had blossomed into a variety of shapes and sizes by the early 1920s. These photos show three designs of the period. **Illus. 362** is a single-seater, here carrying two small children, attached to an A.J.S. motorcycle; the sidecar in **illus. 363** has a dickey seat for an extra passenger, just as in many contemporary small cars. With a third passenger riding pillion it might seem that the motorcycle had a hard task, but as it is a hefty 770cc V-twin B.S.A. no doubt it coped. **Illus. 364** shows a luxurious Mills & Fulford sidecar with tandem seating for two under cover, attached to a Matchless motorcycle.

364. *c.* 1923 Matchless motorcycle with Mills & Fulford sidecar (GB)

365. *c.* 1921 Matchless V-twin motorcycle and sidecar (GB)

This attractive scene in Richmond Park near London features a Matchless V-twin motorcycle and sidecar (**illus. 365**). Note the carriage-type C-springs supporting the sidecar, and spare petrol can between sidecar and motorcycle.

Sidecars were by no means restricted to passenger use, and many were operated by tradesmen who had rapid deliveries to make in heavy traffic. This coachbuilt commercial sidecar (**illus. 366**) is attached to a Phelon & Moore Panther single-cylinder motorcycle of about 1922.

366. *c.* 1922 Phelon & Moore Panther single-cylinder motorcycle with commercial sidecar (GB)

367. 1926 Leyland-B.S.A. motorcycle combination fire engine (GB)

The motorcycle combination fire engine was a rare machine, although a number of companies made them in small numbers, from the early 1900s to at least 1930. **Illus. 367** shows a Leyland-B.S.A. (Leyland equipment with V-twin B.S.A. motorcycle) of 1926 which had a small pumping unit and hoses on the sidecar. The crew of two rode on the motorcycle. Similar machines were made by Merryweather on an A.J.S. motorcycle and by the Hungarian firm, Teudloff-Dittrich, on a Meray motorcycle.

Indian was a familiar name at the International TT races in the Isle of Man from the great day in 1911 when the American make took first three places in the Senior TT. Indians returned after the war and among their riders was Freddie Dixon who was later to achieve fame at the wheel of Riley cars. In **illus. 368** Dixon is seen on an Indian before the 1921 Senior TT.

368. 1921 Indian TT motorcycle (USA)

191

369. 1922 Scott Squirrel 486cc TT motorcycle (GB)

One of the most original, and at the same time commercially successful, motorcycles was the Scott two-stroke, built in Yorkshire by Alfred Angas Scott. He had begun experiments in 1900, but did not put a motorcycle into production until 1909. It had a 3½hp two-stroke twin engine with aircooled barrels and watercooled heads, an open frame, expanding clutch two-speed gear and all-chain drive. Scotts won the 1912 and 1913 TT races and were popular for touring as well as racing. In 1922 came the Squirrel, a 486cc sporting model with light mudguards and dropped handlebars, on which Harry Langman finished 3rd in the Senior TT (**illus. 369**). The basically similar Super Squirrel of 1925 came in two sizes, 496 and 596cc, and was particularly suitable for sidecar work (**illus. 370**). Scott left the company in 1919 and died in 1924, but his two-stroke motorcycles continued to be made until 1950. Early production models were made in the Jowett factory at Bradford.

370. 1925 Scott Super Squirrel motorcycle with sidecar (GB)

Peugeot is the oldest surviving make of motorcycle, for the company built its first machine in 1899, ten years after its first car. In the 1920s Peugeot was particularly known for vertical twins, such as this machine ridden by P. Péah in the 1924 Senior TT (**illus. 371**). In the background is a large Peugeot sleeve-valve touring car.

371. 1924 Peugeot vertical-twin TT motorcycle (F)

372. c. 1926 Brough Superior S.S.80 Special 998cc V-twin motorcycle with sidecar (GB)

Popularly known as the 'Rolls-Royce of motorcycles', the Brough Superior was a beautifully made machine designed and built by George Brough of Nottingham. His father W. E. Brough was also making motorcycles in the same town at the same time, but these were known simply as Broughs, and there was no connection between the two firms. Two of the best-known Brough Superiors were the S.S.80 and S.S.100, both with 998cc V-twin J.A.P. engines, the former side valve, the latter overhead valve. Introduced in 1923 and 1924 respectively, they were both made until the outbreak of war; the last S.S.100 left the factory in April 1940. The S.S.100 was guaranteed to do 100mph, and Brough said in his advertisements, 'A private road, 1¾ miles long, has been very kindly offered to the manufacturer for the purpose of this guarantee.' Both were expensive, 1924 prices being £150 for the 80 and £170 for the 100. **Illus. 372** shows an S.S.80 Special with sidecar, and **illus. 373** an S.S.100, both dating from about 1926.

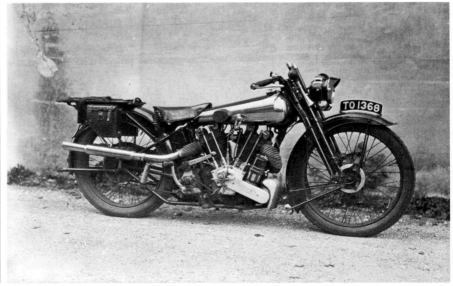

373. c. 1926 Brough Superior S.S.100 998cc V-twin motorcycle (GB)

An attractive-looking and advanced design was the Ascot-Pullin (**illus. 374**), designed by Cyril Pullin and built in the Ascot factory at Letchworth, Hertfordshire, where, briefly, cars were also made. It had a 496cc aircooled flat-twin engine which, with the transmission, was fully enclosed; other features were a welded pressed-steel frame and hydraulic brakes. A windscreen wiper was an optional extra. At £75 it was not over expensive, but its appearance in 1928 came too close to the Depression for it to be a commercial success, and production ended in 1930.

The best-known Swedish motorcycle is the Husqvarna, named after the town, now spelled Huskvarna, where it is made. The first model of 1903 had an F.N. engine, but most subsequent machines have used engines of the company's own manufacture, the largest models being V-twins of up to 1000cc. **Illus. 375** shows two powerful V-twin racing machines before the start of the 1934 Saxtorp races. Between the riders is the designer, Folke Mannerstedt.

374. 1930 Ascot-Pullin 496cc motorcycle (GB)

375. 1934 Husqvarna V-twin racing motorcycles (S)

With Indian, Harley-Davidson was the best-known American motorcycle, achieving countless racing successes, particularly in the 1915–25 period. In the 1930s the best-known Harley-Davidson models were the big V-twins of between 750 and 1200cc. These were, and still are, widely used by Highway Patrols in the United States; **illus. 376** shows a motorcycle 'cop' of the Los Angeles Police with his 1940 radio-equipped Harley-Davidson. In **illus. 377** is a very wide truck adaptation of a mid-1930s 750cc V-twin, in use in Sweden.

Powel Crosley Jr, owner of a radio station on which he was his own disc jockey, and of a football team, the Cincinnati Reds, entered car production in 1939 with a minicar powered by a two-cylinder Waukesha engine. When war came in 1941 he planned to build light motorcycles for the US Army. Only a few prototypes were made, of which one is seen in **illus. 378**. They had flat-twin engines with a car-type gear lever, and the disc wheels were also inherited from Crosley's cars.

377. *c.* 1936 Harley-Davidson 750cc V-twin motorcycle with commercial sidecar (USA)

378. 1941 Crosley 580cc flat-twin motorcycle (USA)

376. 1940 Harley-Davidson V-twin Los Angeles Police motorcycle (USA)

BICYCLES TRICYCLES AND QUADRICYCLES

INTRODUCTION

Considering the simplicity of the idea, it is surprising that the bicycle did not arrive earlier in history than it did, for the first appearance of a two-wheeled man-propelled vehicle was in 1790 when the Comte de Sivrac demonstrated to Parisians the machine he called a *célerifère*. This took the form of a wooden horse with two wheels, propelled by the feet along the ground. Despite its lack of any form of steering it achieved some popularity in Paris, and races were held along the Champs Elysées. The next important step was taken by the German Baron Drais von Sauerbronn who made a steerable *vélocifère*, as they were now called, in 1817. He dispensed with the frivolity of the horse's head, and in addition to the steerable front wheel he provided himself with a cushioned saddle and a rest for the arms and chest. This vehicle was obviously of more practical use than anything previously seen, and when he brought it to Paris in 1818 it immediately became even more of a sensation than de Sivrac's *célerifère* had been. Christened the Draisine, or Draisienne, it came to England in the same year, and under the name pedestrian curricle, or more popularly hobby horse, a considerable number were sold to Regency bucks, and ladies' models were also made. The craze was very short-lived, however, because it was a fashionable novelty rather than a practical means of transport, and because of the incidence of hernia among over-enthusiastic riders.

The first man to apply pedals to a two-wheeler was an obscure Scottish blacksmith, Kirkpatrick Macmillan, who in 1839 made what was the ancestor of the modern bicycle. It had wooden treadles suspended from the steering head, which were linked via connecting rods and cranks to the rear wheel. Macmillan is said to have achieved speeds of 14mph on his machine, and to have ridden up to 40 miles at a stretch, but he did not make any for sale. Perhaps it was too much of a novelty, the Scots being less given to passing fads than Londoners, or perhaps Macmillan was simply not interested in becoming a manufacturer. The first bicycles made for sale came from Paris, and were in a way a retrograde step from Macmillan's machine, for they had direct drive from the pedals to the front wheel. Built by a coach repairer, Pierre Michaux, with his sons Henri and

Ernest, the first velocipedes appeared in 1861. By 1865 the firm of Michaux had built a special factory for this work and was making 400 per year. Originally the front wheel was only slightly larger than the rear one, but gradually the size of the front wheel was increased in order to allow higher speeds (through higher gearing) and reduce the power of potholes to throw the rider off. Of course the larger wheel had the disadvantage that if the rider was thrown, he had that much further to fall, but the skilful rider prided himself that such a thing would not happen, and the larger the wheel the greater the self-esteem of the rider. In 1870 the so-called penny farthing appeared, although this name was not used for twenty years or so, by which time the design was obsolescent, being succeeded by the Safety bicycle. The usual name was high-wheel, or Ordinary, bicycle. Like the Michaux 'boneshaker', the Ordinary was driven directly on the front wheel which could be as large as 60in in diameter, although a more normal size was 54in. The rear wheel averaged 17in. Although their use was restricted to young and fairly athletic riders, the Ordinaries became very popular during the 1870s, and it was estimated that there were at least 50,000 of them on the roads of England by 1877, made by about thirty manufacturers. They were also popular in the United States, where a variation was the Star bicycle in which the large driven wheel was at the rear.

The inherent danger of the Ordinary led to a considerable vogue for the tricycle, which appeared in the mid-1870s and was made in bewildering variety for about fifteen years. Most had two large driving wheels and a small stabilizing wheel at the front or rear; occasionally there were two stabilizers, making the machine a quadricycle, and the front or rear wheel could be detached at will. One of these designs was James Starley's Salvo Quad, of which Queen Victoria ordered two when she was staying on the Isle of Wight in 1881. The use of two driven wheels led to the adoption of the differential gear, but before this some tricycles were made with one large driven wheel at the side, and two smaller ones on the opposite side. Examples of these were the Humber and Coventry Lever tricycles. Quite a number of tricycles were made to seat two people, either in tandem or side by side. The latter were known as sociables or, in Starley's case, as the Honeymoon Wonder. After about 1890 tricycles began to decline in popularity with the coming of the Safety bicycle, but they continued to be made, in a form still familiar today on children's models, with a single front wheel and two driven rear ones, all of the same size.

The most important development in spreading the popularity of the bicycle was undoubtedly the invention of the Safety cycle, coupled with the pneumatic tyre which arrived on the scene shortly afterwards. The characteristics of the Safety were small wheels (not of the same size at first, although they soon came to be so), and chain drive to the rear wheel. B.S.A. made a Safety in 1884, but the design that really led to the modern bicycle was John Kemp Starley's Rover Safety of 1885, in which the wheels were of nearly equal size, and steering was direct from the handlebars to the wheel. By 1890 the diamond-frame bicycle with equal-sized wheels and pneumatic tyres had arrived, and the boom was on. In America, production rose from under 200,000 in 1889 to over a million ten years later, and in most industrialized countries bicycle factories flourished, giving employment to thousands and establishing a framework from which the motor industry was to grow a few years later.

Although there had been a few lady tricyclists, and even a select band who rode Ordinaries, it was the Safety bicycle that put women on wheels in a big way, and encouraged emancipation. With a bicycle a girl could slip away from her chaperone 'to keep a secret tryst with her lover, and still be home for afternoon tea while innocently protesting that she had just been . . . to collect wild flowers to press'.

Such a degree of independence was not popular with conservative folk of either sex at first, although a magazine grudgingly replied to a girl who enquired about the propriety of bicycling that 'The mere act of riding a bicycle is not in itself sinful, and if it is the only means of reaching the church on a Sunday, it may be excusable.' What to wear presented a problem, and those women who took to 'Rational Dress' (knickerbockers and long leggings) faced ridicule, hostile jibes and the possibility that a hotel would refuse to serve them. This happened to Lady Harberton in 1896, and although the landlady was taken to court she was acquitted.

An important development that took some time to become widespread was the free wheel, by means of which the pedals remained still while the bicycle sped along. This was invented in 1881, but was not widely used until after the turn of the century, largely because brakes were sketchy or non-existent on the early Safeties, and the usual method of braking was by back-pedalling. It is surprising that the rod- or cable-operated rim brake was not used earlier, for back-pedalling with fixed pedals must have been dangerous as well as uncomfortable if the machine was travelling at all fast. Another improvement which came in at the turn of the century was the variable-speed gear, in particular the three-speed Sturmey-Archer. By 1905 a good-quality bicycle had all the components of its descendants of the 1920s and 1930s, and there is little that can be said about the history of the bicycle until the coming of the small-wheel Moulton-type machine in the 1960s, which is beyond the scope of this book.

379. 1819 hobby horse in 1907 (GB)

381. c. 1869 Michaux velocipedes (F)

383. 1897 line-up of Ordinaries in America

The first improvement on the original two-wheeled *célerifère* was made by the German Baron Drais von Sauerbronn who made a steerable machine in 1817. Known as the Draisienne in France and the hobby horse in England, it achieved rapid popularity and models for both ladies and gentlemen were made. The photo (**illus. 379**), taken in 1907, shows a hobby horse of about 1819 with the Malvern cyclemaker W. R. Santler.

One of the many early attempts at self-propulsion was the Aellopedes tricycle (**illus. 380**), built by Mr Revis, a mathematician of Cambridge, in 1839. Operated by treadles connected to the rear axle, it had driving wheels over 6ft in diameter. It had a claimed speed of 20 to 30mph, which seems most unlikely, and Mr Revis offered his design to the Post Office, 'with a view to the speedier and more economical transmission of the cross-mails'

The first men to commercialize the bicycle were Pierre and Henri Michaux, Parisian coach repairers who made their first velocipede in 1861, and turned out nearly 400 four years later. The new machines became as fashionable in Paris as the hobby horse had been forty years before and arrived in England in 1868. **Illus. 381** shows the Prince Imperial and his cousin trying a pair of Michaux velocipedes in the reserved garden of the Tuileries, while his father the Emperor Napoleon III (far left) watches.

380. 1839 Aellopedes self-propulsion tricycle (GB)

The high-wheel, or Ordinary, bicycle appeared in 1870, and soon established itself as the standard machine, ousting the velocipede within a few years. The large driving wheel had a gearing-up effect; the rear wheel was only a stabilizer. Some Ordinaries had front wheels with a 60in diameter, but a more normal size was 50 to 54in. The nickname 'penny farthing' did not come into use until the Ordinary was on its way out, replaced by the Safety. **Illus. 382**, a photo taken in about 1887 at Malvern, Worcestershire, shows the Santler brothers with two Ordinaries and a tricycle.

A line-up of Ordinaries and their riders (**illus. 383**) on the occasion of one of America's first organized bicycle tours, outside Readsville, Mass., in September 1879. The first rider is the noted bicycle author, Charles E. Pratt. Next to him is Colonel Albert Pope, maker of the Columbia bicycle and, later, of passenger cars such as the Pope-Hartford and Pope-Toledo.

382. Bicycles at Malvern, c. 1887 (GB)

384. 1879 Singer Challenge tricycle (GB)

The tricycle achieved great popularity during the heyday of the Ordinary bicycle because the latter required a courageous and athletic rider, and was quite unsuitable for the elderly or for women. The first production tricycle appeared in 1876 and within five years a bewildering variety was seen. Some had the single wheel at the front, others had it at the rear; others such as the Humber and Coventry Lever tricycles had two small wheels in line, and a larger one at the side. Some tricycles carried two people in tandem. A popular model was the 'Sociable', in which the two passengers sat side by side, and luggage could be carried at the rear. However, as tricycles became more complicated so they

386. c. 1886 tricycle (GB)

became heavier, and with the coming of the Safety bicycle they began to lose their popularity. The photographs show a lever-steered Singer Challenge tricycle of 1879 (**illus. 384**); an American Sociable of the 1880s (**illus. 385**); and a tricycle of about the same date ridden by S. Hill, Sub-Captain of the Worcester Tricycle Club (**illus. 386**). Note the oil lamps, and the horn carried by Mr Hill.

A tandem convertible quadricycle roadster of about 1885 (**illus. 388**). Made by the Coventry Machinists' Co. Ltd, this machine could be converted into a single tricycle by detaching either the front or rear wheels. This example was photographed behind the White House, Washington D.C.

Titled 'Wheeling on Riverside Drive', this engraving (**illus. 389**) from *Harper's Weekly* of July 1886 shows a Sociable tricycle of the type known in Britain as the Honeymoon Wonder, and behind it an Ordinary bicycle and a tandem tricycle.

385. 1880s American Sociable (USA)

388. *c.* 1885 Coventry Machinists' tandem quadricycle (GB)

389. 1886 Sociable tricycle, with an Ordinary bicycle and a tandem tricycle (USA)

387. *c.* 1890 Rover tricycle (GB)

Illus. 387 shows a very much more modern-looking tricycle, of a type made into the first decade of the twentieth century, and still familiar in children's machines today. It is a Rover of about 1890.

207

390. 1893 Valère racing tricycle (F)

391. 1896 Safety bicycle adapted to carry the steersman and four passengers (USA)

392. c. 1890 tandem bicycle with two children's tricycles (GB)

An unconventional racing tricycle of 1893 (**illus. 390**), designed and built by a Frenchman, M. Valère, who was a noted oarsman as well as a cyclist. It is both manually and foot operated, M. Valere's idea being that as he pedalled so his arms naturally moved forward and backward, so why not harness this additional source of power? Although his machine weighed more than twice as much as the lightest of conventional tricycles, he covered 500m (547yd) in 45sec on the machine's first test.

A 'bicycle made for two' was one thing, but this obliging paterfamilias, H. J. vom Scheidt of Buffalo, N.Y., carried no fewer than four of his offspring on an adapted Safety bicycle in 1896 (**illus. 391**). The rearmost child has a saddle, but the others sit on canvas and the front pair must turn in the direction of the steering.

The tandem bicycle was developed in England by Dan Albone of Biggleswade, Bedfordshire, in 1886, although there had been earlier experiments with tandem Ordinaries. Albone's original tandem had coupled steering for both handlebars and a single diagonal backbone. The tandem bicycle in **illus. 392** has this backbone, which made it particularly suitable for women riders. Also in this photograph, which dates from about 1890, are two children's tricycles, one of them a tandem, and three Ordinary bicycles leaning against the walls in the background. **Illus. 393** shows a more modern tandem of 1896 with the double-diamond frame that became standard design for tandems. Note that pneumatic tyres had arrived by this date.

The Safety bicycle with relatively small equal-sized wheels was the machine that really made cycling a world-wide popular pastime and gradually drove from the roads both the Ordinary bicycle and the tricycle. The first Safeties of 1884 had solid tyres, which made for serious vibration. But with the coming of the Dunlop pneumatic tyre in 1888 the way was open for the cycle boom of the 1890s which made several fortunes, such as those of Adolphe Clément in France and Colonel Albert Pope in America, and laid the foundations of the motor industry. **Illus. 394** shows three Worcestershire cyclists with early Safeties, *c.* 1892.

393. 1896 double-diamond-frame tandem (GB)

394. c. 1892 Safety bicycles (GB)

209

395. 1895 amphibious tricycle built by H. Savage of Worcester (GB)

396. c. 1902 ladies' bicycle with loop frame (GB)

In the early 1890s there was a rash of bicycle boats, from simple catamarans, the ancestors of today's pedal boats, to quite substantial craft that looked like small steamboats. There were also a few amphibians such as this tricycle (**illus. 395**) built by H. Savage of Worcester in 1895. It was pedalled for some distance up the River Severn and then ridden onto dry land.

An early group of Safety cyclists using rail attachments (**illus. 397**), seen on a spur line of the Pittsburg & Western Railroad between Cluffs Mills and McCrays, Pa., in the 1890s

Cycling dress for women caused much comment and argument in the 1890s. A lady could wear Rational Dress which consisted of knickerbockers and long leggings with a coat designed to conceal as much as possible of these garments, but this attire often caused hostility. The alternative was a long skirt such as the one seen in **illus. 396**, which dictated the loop frame of the bicycle and also such practical developments as the enclosed chaincase.

397. c. 1895 Safety bicycles (USA)

The tandem was the largest bicycle used for
normal pleasure purposes, but for racing
larger machines were made, such as this
Rudge quadruplet of 1895 (**illus. 398**). Third
from the left is W. J. Bladder, the Worcester
bicyclemaker who was in business from 1893
to the early 1920s.

Dropped handlebars first appeared in the
1890s and soon became standardized for
sporting machines. **Illus. 400** shows
J. H. Johnson, winner of the Lincolnshire
Road Race Association's 50-mile John Bull
Cup, on his Rudge-Whitworth in 1925.
Supporting him is his brother, T. W.
Johnson.

398. 1895 Rudge racing quadruplet (GB)

400. 1925 Rudge-Whitworth racing bicycle (GB)

The composer Sir Edward Elgar with his
brand-new Sunbeam bicycle in the spring of
1903 (**illus. 399**). Note the three brakes and
the watch holder on the handlebars. By
this date the bicycle had reached a standard
form of design it was to retain, except for
modifications and adaptations, notably for
racing, for the next fifty years or so.

399. 1903 Sunbeam bicycle with its owner, Sir Edward Elgar (GB)

BRITISH AND AMERICAN EQUIVALENT TERMS

ABBREVIATIONS

For the convenience of readers a short glossary of British and American terms is given below. The list is less than comprehensive because the meaning of many technical terms peculiar either to British or to American usage, or belonging to the earlier years of automotive and cycling history, can be gathered from their contexts in the book.

articulated vehicle ('artic')	tractor and semi-trailer
bonnet	hood
boot	trunk
capacity (of engine)	displacement
coupé de ville	town car
dickey	rumble seat
dustcart	garbage truck
engine	motor
epicyclic (gearbox)	planetary (transmission)
estate car	station wagon
gearbox	transmission
hood	top
lorry	truck
mudguard	fender
petrol	gasoline
refuse collector	garbage truck
saloon	sedan
sedanca de ville	town car
shooting brake	station wagon
tram(~way)	streetcar (line)
two-stroke	two-cycle
van	panel delivery
windscreen	windshield
wing	fender

bhp	brake horsepower
cc	cubic centimetre(s) (1cc = 0·0610237ci)
ci	cubic inch(es) (1ci = 16·3871cc)
CV	*cheval- (cheveaux-) vapeur*. French: horsepower
cwt	hundredweight(s) (in Britain, where it often expresses load-carrying capacity, 1cwt = 112lb)
ft	foot (feet)
hp	horsepower
in	inch(es)
lb	pound(s)
min	minute(s)
ohc	overhead camshaft(s)
ohv	overhead valve(s)
PS	*Pferdestärke(n)*. German: horsepower
rpm	revolutions per minute
sec	second(s)
sv	side valve(s)
TT	Tourist Trophy

Countries of manufacture are indicated by their recognized International Registration Letters, as follows:

A	Austria
AUS	Australia
CDN	Canada
CH	Switzerland
CS	Czechoslovakia
D	Germany
DK	Denmark
F	France
GB	Great Britain and Northern Ireland
H	Hungary
I	Italy
S	Sweden
SU	Union of Soviet Socialist Republics (used here to include pre-1917 Russia)
USA	United States of America

213

Horse-drawn vehicles in London's
Cheapside in 1907 with, in the middle
distance, a solitary car.

ILLUSTRATION SOURCES

The illustrations in this book are from the National Motor Museum, Beaulieu, Hampshire, with the exception of those from the museums, libraries, journals and individuals listed below, to whom the authors wish to express their gratitude. Apologies are offered for any inadvertent omissions from this list.

38	Margus-Hans Kuuse
53	Automotive History Collection, Detroit Public Library
66	B. H. Vanderveen Collection
68	Radio Times Hulton Picture Library
76	Zora Arkus-Duntov
87	Vačlav Petrik Collection
88	Vačlav Petrik Collection
90	Vačlav Petrik Collection
92	G. N. Georgano Collection
95	Margus-Hans Kuuse
104	Vačlav Petrik Collection
141	Arthur Ingram Collection
149	Philadelphia Free Library
151	Margus-Hans Kuuse
160	Björn-Eric Lindh
161	Monty Bowers
178	Peter Roberts Collection
183	Vačlav Petrik Collection
189	G. N. Georgano Collection
191	Vačlav Petrik Collection
194	Vačlav Petrik Collection
199	*Old Motor Magazine*
204	John Montville Collection
207	John Montville Collection
214	Arthur Ingram Collection
215	Arthur Ingram Collection
216	*Old Motor Magazine*
217	Peter Roberts Collection
220	Arthur Ingram Collection
221	Arthur Ingram Collection
223	Arthur Ingram Collection
224	Arthur Ingram Collection
229	Ford of Canada
233	Arthur Ingram Collection
234	John Montville Collection
235	Twin Coach photo: courtesy Motor Bus Society
236	John Montville Collection
237	Ford of Canada
239	Vačlav Petrik Collection
241	Arthur Ingram Collection
243	Margus-Hans Kuuse
244	Arthur Ingram Collection
245	Arthur Ingram Collection
255	Arthur Ingram Collection
256	Vačlav Petrik Collection
258	John Montville Collection
261	Arthur Ingram Collection
262	Arthur Ingram Collection
264	Arthur Ingram Collection
265	John Montville Collection
267	Arthur Ingram Collection
270	Arthur Ingram Collection
272	Jean-Claude Labreque
273	Arthur Ingram Collection
274	Arthur Ingram Collection
275	Arthur Ingram Collection
277	Peter Roberts Collection
278	Arthur Ingram Collection
279	R. E. Graham Collection
280	Arthur Ingram Collection
281	Arthur Ingram Collection
282	Sven Bengtson Collection
285	Arthur Ingram Collection
287	Arthur Ingram Collection
288	Sven Bengtson Collection
289	Arthur Ingram Collection
290	Arthur Ingram Collection
292	John Montville Collection
293	Arthur Ingram Collection
300	Peter Roberts Collection
301	Philadelphia Free Library
302	G. N. Georgano Collection
303	Olyslager Auto Library
312	Motor Bus Society
313	Radio Times Hulton Picture Library
315	*Old Motor Magazine*
317	Motor Bus Society
320	Motor Bus Society
322	London Transport Executive
323	London Transport Executive
324	London Transport Executive
325	London Transport Executive
326	Motor Bus Society
327	Twin Coach photo: courtesy Motor Bus Society
334	Motor Bus Society
336	*Old Motor Magazine*
337	Hans-Otto Neubauer Collection
339	Greyhound photo: courtesy Motor Bus Society
340	Deutsches Zweiradmuseum, Neckarsulm
341	Deutsches Zweiradmuseum, Neckarsulm
352	*Old Motor Magazine*
355	A. B. Demaus Collection
359	*Old Motor Magazine*
360	*Old Motor Magazine*
361	*Old Motor Magazine*
362	A. B. Demaus Collection
363	*Old Motor Magazine*
364	*Old Motor Magazine*
365	*Old Motor Magazine*
366	*Old Motor Magazine*
367	Arthur Ingram Collection
377	*Old Motor Magazine*
379	A. B. Demaus Collection
380	Mary Evans Picture Library
381	Mary Evans Picture Library
382	A. B. Demaus Collection
383	Smithsonian Institution, Washington D.C.
385	Smithsonian Institution, Washington D.C.
386	A. B. Demaus Collection
387	A. B. Demaus Collection
388	Smithsonian Institution, Washington D.C.
389	Smithsonian Institution, Washington D.C.
390	Mary Evans Picture Library
391	Mary Evans Picture Library
392	A. B. Demaus Collection
393	A. B. Demaus Collection
394	A. B. Demaus Collection
395	A. B. Demaus Collection
396	A. B. Demaus Collection
397	Smithsonian Institution, Washington D.C.
398	A. B. Demaus Collection
399	A. B. Demaus Collection
400	Derek Roberts/Southern Veteran Cycle Club

In the seven years since the picture on page 214 was taken Unic taxicabs replaced the horse-drawn cab on London's streets.

INDEX OF NAMES

Roman numerals refer to captions to colour pictures